GOOD HOUSEKEEPING
CARAVAN COOKING

GOOD HOUSEKEEPING
CARAVAN COOKING

Compiled by
GOOD HOUSEKEEPING INSTITUTE

Published in association with

RAC

EBURY PRESS
London

First published in Great Britain by Ebury Press
Chestergate House, Vauxhall Bridge Road
London SW1V 1HF

First impression 1977

ISBN 0 85223 120 2

Editor Amanda Atha
Home economist Janet Marsh
Illustrations by Hilary Evans
Cover design by Glenn Steward

Filmset and printed in Great Britain by
BAS Printers Limited, Over Wallop, Hampshire
and bound by
G & J Kitcat Ltd
Shand Street, London SE1

Contents

To help you see at a glance which recipes can be made on your cooking equipment we have marked each recipe with a symbol as follows:

one burner   two burners

one burner   two burners
plus grill   plus grill

No symbol means no cooking is needed

**Each recipe serves four people
unless otherwise stated**

Foreword

For a family holiday, caravanning takes a lot of beating. It gives freedom to go where you like, to search for better weather or a better beach and to explore places you might never see if you were bound by package deals and hotels.

Experienced caravanners and campers are normally very well planned people. An attitude which is too free and easy will probably result in a shambles and frayed tempers so it's worth selecting equipment carefully and deciding to make varied and interesting meals. That's what this little book is all about. Firstly there's sound advice about choosing a caravan, and camping equipment and planning space to the best advantage, not forgetting safety precautions. Then GHI has collected, adapted and tested recipes which are all quick and easy to cook but far removed from the campers traditional bangers and beans. Devilled Chicken with Rice, Pan Pizza, Burgundy Beef are just a few examples of the dishes we've cooked on caravan and camping stoves. Each recipe shows clearly whether you need one or two burners or a grill. There's a particularly mouthwatering section which gives ideas for using hedgerow fruits and berries, fungi and locally caught fish.

The RAC with all their expertise in touring and caravanning have given us invaluable help in compiling this book.

If you have any queries about the recipes the GHI's experts will be glad to answer them. Write to Good Housekeeping Institute, Chestergate House, Vauxhall Bridge Road, London SW1V 1HF.

CAROL MACARTNEY

Cooking in a caravan

The first step to perfect caravan cooking is to pick the right van – one tailored to your personal needs. If you have decided to buy a motorcaravan* or trailer tent (a kind of folding caravan), there is not much choice between different kitchen designs since the basic layout of both is pretty standard. A few motorcaravans have an end kitchen, but the majority, like trailer caravans, have all the cooking appliances and sink along one side of the vehicle, whereas most trailer tents have any cooking appliance that may be installed at one end.

Kitchen position
However, if you are going to invest in a trailer caravan (and they are immeasurably better for cooking purposes) there is an immediate choice to be made between a kitchen at one end or in the middle of the design. If the family is planning to take the van out as much as possible, and you are, therefore, going to be involved in a fair amount of van cooking, it is marginally better to choose an end kitchen. With a central kitchen you are in the thick of the living area and therefore the chances are that you will be making that special *entrée* with a constant stream of traffic going to and fro from one end of the van to the other. With an end kitchen, all your equipment and working surfaces are located away from the living area and the only 'through' traffic will be in and out of the van itself.

It used to be considered preferable to have a central kitchen for towing purposes because when a car is pulling a van, the trailer should be loaded with the heavy items over the axle in the middle of the van, and the heaviest items in most vans are the cooker, refrigerator, cupboards, canned food, etc. However, modern vans are much better designed than their predecessors and this consideration need not influence you in the choice of kitchen location.

---

* Trailer caravans, folding caravans and tent trailers carry VAT at $12\frac{1}{2}\%$ on the selling price. Motorcaravans carry car tax at 10% and VAT at 8%.

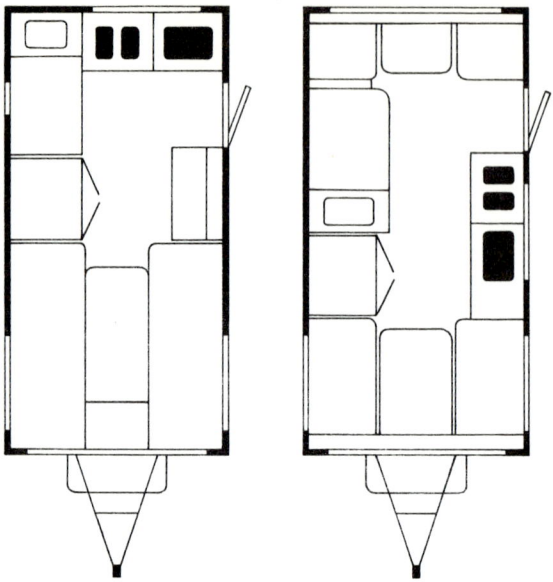

Caravan layout showing end and side kitchens

Working surfaces, storage space

Even the most enthusiastic caravanner would admit that the
working surfaces in trailers are limited – and those in
motorcaravans even more so. Generally all that is available is a
hinged working top over the burners and grill and another
over the sink (often combined into one unit); the top of a
cupboard or refrigerator and one or two tables – although this
depends on the size of the van. In these conditions obviously
meal preparation must be finished or nearly finished before
one starts cooking, since a whole working surface is normally
'lost' once the gas burners are lit. In some vans, the flaps are
hinged in such a way that it is possible to turn the work
surface and continue to use it even when the sink or cooker is
also in use.

Storage space is a little more generous (and quite ingenious),
with cupboards under the work units, crockery and cutlery
drawers and lockers and perhaps a further cupboard, together
with various lengths of shelving. You might think that the
larger the van, the larger the storage space and working tops

but it does not always work out like this; the extra square footage in the larger vans may be taken up by lavish seating and sleeping accommodation and further storage space at the living end of the van, away from the cooking area.

Once you have chosen the position of the kitchen the main thing to look for is the standard of workmanship and here, as usual, you get what you pay for. The higher priced vans have a much better standard of finish. But when visiting dealers and examining different models, look for irritating gaps between working surfaces where crumbs or liquids could slip down into uncleanable recesses; test doors to cupboards and door catches, as bad workmanship or bad design will lead to storage unit doors flying open and disgorging their contents all over the floor. (Remember that a van under tow has considerable stress placed on its built-in units.) Avoid vans with 'lost' storage space below units, for it will infuriate you every time you gaze at those wasted cubic inches. Make sure that all cupboard shelves are lipped; this refinement stops heavy articles thudding against the door so hard that it is forced open.

Kitchen positioned at the end of the caravan

Stainless steel unit combining sink, drainer and cooker

Cooking facilities: hobs and ovens

Most tourers, both motorcaravan and trailer, leave the factory equipped with a two-burner hob unit and a grill. The units have three push-in-and-turn knobs for turning on the gas to burners and grill, a non-spill chrome support on which you place your pots and pans (the support is detachable for easy cleaning), and usually they come complete with a grill pan. Using only this basic equipment you are restricted to food that can be stewed, boiled, fried, grilled or steamed; you will have to ignore any menus that talk of roasting or baking. Not only that but you only have half the number of burners of the normal, domestic cooker and the grill is also a scaled-down version of the domestic type (an average hob or cooker would measure about $43 \times 35 \times 18$ cm ($17 \times 14 \times 7$ in)). As most caravan manufacturers offer an oven as an optional extra, consider having one installed when you make the purchase. But if you are undecided about the merits of an oven you can always have one installed at a later date or, indeed, fit it yourself. Most tourer-makers design the kitchen cupboards so that the one below the burners is already the right size and shape to take most oven designs on the market.

There are about twelve manufacturers of ovens; many of them make a combined unit of burners and oven, a popular choice. If your van has a one-piece stainless steel top, in which the burners are incorporated with a drainer and sink, you will have to settle for a separate oven if adding it at a later date, unless you're prepared to organise extensive rebuilding. Most of the ovens available on the market are big enough to take a $1 \cdot 3 – 1 \cdot 8$-kg (3–4-lb) bird – dimensions are about $35 \times 44 \times 43$ cm ($14 \times 17\frac{1}{2} \times 17$ in) – and some come with a flame failure device for a few extra pounds. They usually have a drop-down door.

The brand leaders in the caravan market are British: there are some imported ovens, but they are difficult to obtain and spares may not be as easily obtainable as with the British models.

For those who are not anxious to lose cupboard space by having an oven installed and yet want more than two burners, there are some alternatives. For instance, there are a few large hobs available. They might be a little awkward to fit yourself, but the final result of three or four burners instead of two could make it worthwhile. Or you could install a second hob, especially one without a grill, which would take up little space. (One caravan manufacturer has been fitting two hobs as standard for some time and the idea is proving popular.) You can even buy an oven which works by placing it on the burners and using their heat to build up the oven temperature. The appliance, sold by Joy & King, measures 28 × 28 × 23 cm (11 × 11 × 9 in) and is fitted with two shelves. It costs less than a third of the price of a traditional caravan oven, and has the advantage of not taking up valuable cupboard space. Of course, one cannot use it at the same time as the burners, but it is certainly handy for heating pies, making casseroles, etc. A similar American-made oven actually folds flat to a depth of 5 cm (2 in) when not in use. Its normal dimensions are 29 × 29 × 30 cm (11½ × 11½ × 12 in); its folded size is 29 × 5 × 30 cm (11½ × 2 × 12 in). This Coleman oven also has a heat gauge on the door. It works on exactly the same principle as the Joy & King oven but costs more than twice as much.

Supplementary cooking facilities

If you think you might need an extra burner just occasionally – for that special Saturday night slap-up dinner perhaps – you can always buy a small single burner camping stove which is fuelled by a small gas cartridge. The cooking section screws directly on to the fuel supply. An advantage of this appliance is its portability: you can take it with you on picnics. The camping stove often has a windshield, a stabilising base for use on uneven or rocky ground, and comes complete with a carry-tin. There is enough gas in the disposable cartridge to last for a number of meals. A trip to your local camping shop will reveal a vast range of one- or two-burner portable cookers.

*Cooking unit
with hood and
folding worktop*

Smells and ventilation

Whether or not you have extra cooking appliances you might find that a cooker hood is a good investment. Indeed, many caravan manufacturers in the middle to upper price bracket already fit a hood as standard. The best known is made by Westool who offer two models, the Standard and the Concord. The purpose-built 12v DC cooker hoods remove cooking odours and steam at an electric consumption of only 0·65 amps. Installation usually involves fitting the hood either below or actually in the kitchen roof locker and cutting through the sidewall to an external vent. Alternatively, you could consider installing extra ventilation – for although British Standard 4626 lays down minimum requirements for the ventilation facilities in touring caravans, a little extra will surely never go amiss.

Installing extra ventilation is cheaper – about half the price – than investing in a cooker hood. The most popular model is the Electrolux vent, a non-motorised device which works on a vacuum principle. The airflow outside the van, even on a windless day, creates a partial vacuum within the vent, thus causing air to rush into the vacuum. The vent is draught and insect-proof and simple to install. Similar units are offered by one or two other manufacturers, or you can buy an extractor fan unit, or combine a fan with a vent. Fitting an extra rooflight is an ambitious way to get extra ventilation. Whatever kind of ventilation is installed, the object is the same – to remove stale air and replace it with fresh: clearly, you have to induce fresh air into the caravan to replace the extracted air, so a fresh air inlet should always be fitted.

Refrigerators

The other major decision to be taken involving an installed appliance is to decide whether or not you need a refrigerator. Many caravanners, especially those who frequently tour abroad, consider a refrigerator a 'must'; others regard it as unnecessary and more trouble than it's worth. The advantages of having a refrigerator are obvious – a wider choice of menu involving chilling dishes, storing commercially frozen food, a cold area to keep foods fresh and a supply of ice-cubes. The disadvantages are that a caravan fridge does cost a lot – especially when compared with the price of a comparable domestic model – and you do lose some storage space. Also, caravan fridges tend to give trouble, though most complaints can usually be traced to poor installation, inadequate ventilation or misuse.

As with fitting an oven, it is easier to install a refrigerator at the time of purchasing your van than to have it installed later. It is possible to put in a fridge yourself if you are well-versed in gas fittings and electrical connections. Manufacturers usually supply full fitting instructions with the device. But in view of the fact that most fridge problems arise from poor installation, it is unquestionably better to let an expert tackle the job. Most models run on bottled gas or from a 12v battery. Whichever source of power is used the cooling unit produces heat and the whole point of a refrigerator is to lower the temperature within. Therefore the generated heat must be dispersed and adequate ventilation around the appliance is vital. The clearance below, behind and above the refrigerator for ventilation of the cooling unit must never be reduced or the air flow will be impeded.

Similarly, when running the fridge on bottled gas, burnt gases are given off which must be vented to the outside of the caravan. Therefore it is imperative to fit a flue kit and vents, and these must be in the correct position to allow the gases to escape. Fitting a refrigerator into a van is not an easy proposition, but once properly installed it will keep working in a surrounding temperature of up to 32°C (90°F).

There are few manufacturers of caravan refrigerators. The most popular model is undoubtedly the Electrolux RM120 and most tourer kitchen units have a suitable recess to accommodate it. The RM120 can be built into a cupboard base unit (the door of the cupboard has to be removed for adequate ventilation), beneath a worktop or sink unit, or at waist-height in a suitable cupboard unit. It has a flint lighter and a built-in safety device to ensure that if the flame is extinguished, the gas is automatically turned off. In a room temperature of 25°C (77°F) the refrigerator will burn 213 g (0·47 lb) liquid in 24 hours, less if the air in the van is cooler. When running it on a 12v battery, the model consumes 7 amps. The door can be altered from righthand to lefthand opening if desired, the storage arrangements inside are versatile (four half-shelves which can be used together or separately) and the internal volume is 27·8 litres (1 cu ft) gross.

Having a fridge which will run off a 12v battery *or* bottled gas is a great asset. If you run it off bottled gas while towing the van, the chances are that the flame will be extinguished and the gas cut off long before you reach your destination. Also, you should stop the refrigerator every time you pull into a service station to comply with regulations which forbid you to take a naked flame near petrol pumps.

The 12v circuit is only meant to maintain temperature. The idea is that you pre-cool the refrigerator on bottled gas for several hours before departure and then switch to the 12v system when towing. Once you are stationary again on a caravan site you should switch back to gas. It would be virtually impossible to run a caravan fridge continuously on 12v only because of the high current consumption; a 40 amp battery would be as flat as the proverbial pancake in less than five hours. It might also prove dangerous as the 12v circuit does not have a thermostat to regulate temperature.

The other popular refrigerator on the British market is the de-luxe Electrolux RM212 which has the added advantage of a two-star frozen food compartment. (Naturally enough, it costs more than its standard counterpart.) With its internal volume of 56 litres (2 cu ft) this model has two full-width shelves and two door-shelves, the lower one capable of taking four pints of milk. The unit uses slightly more gas and electricity, 308 g

(0·68 lb) liquid/24 hours at maximum control setting and 8 amps, because of its larger size. It will also run off 220–240v mains electricity and so would act as a substitute if your domestic refrigerator was out of commission. Some Continental sites and a handful of British ones provide power supplies.

As with other van fridges – with the exception of one expensive imported model – the Electrolux models only work efficiently when the van is pitched on a level or near-level piece of ground. A permanent list of more than 2–3° in any direction will probably interfere with its operation (besides making sure that you fall out of bed and your cup of tea slides off the table on to the floor). If the refrigerator does stop working it is often possible to start it again by placing a large block of ice in it – in emergency, use a packet of frozen vegetables. Keeping the gas jet free from dust will also help to ensure trouble-free running.

Other cooling methods
If you have decided that there is not enough room in your caravan for a refrigerator but you still want some kind of cooling unit, you might consider investing in a free-standing camping box. These portable refrigerators, which are ideal for chilling drinks and keeping perishables fresh, normally have a three-way operation: 220–240v mains electricity, 12v car battery for use when travelling, and bottled gas. A typical camping box, again made by Electrolux, is the RC150 which

Making more space with a caravan awning

has an internal volume of 30·6 litres (1·08 cu ft) and measures
42 × 51 × 42 cm (16½ × 20 × 16½ in).

Again, this type of fridge should be kept away from any heat
source and should also be kept level but, most important, it
must not be run off bottled gas inside the caravan or, indeed, in
any enclosed space. The reason for this inflexible rule is that
camping boxes do not have a flue to dispose of the products of
combustion. The gases given off have to be dispersed by
currents of air and so the unit must be run in the open air. It
must not be enclosed in any way. Most caravanners who have a
camping box run it in their awning (a kind of tent with three
sides only, the fourth side being the side of the van) or annexe
(the same sort of tent normally used in conjunction with a
motorcaravan).

Keeping food cool without a fridge

There are other ways and means of keeping food cool, but these
will not lower temperatures to any significant extent. All they
will do is maintain the existing temperature for a few hours.
You can keep produce cool outside. The old trick of immersing
bottles of milk, cordial, etc in a running stream still works and
you can also store food in the shade underneath your van if you
are not staying on a formal site where the practice might be
frowned on. The food flask that can be used as a hay box works
just as well at keeping food cold; butter will stay firm in the
flask and can be sliced off as required. For cold drinks, put a
supply of ice-cubes * in the flask before you add the drink. Then
store under the van if possible, or in the refrigerator if there is
enough room. For the caravanner who does not have a fridge,
or for the one who does have a powered cooling unit but wants
extra cold storage, there are various insulated containers and
cool bags on the market. They range from the large
39 × 22 × 25 cm (15¼ × 8½ × 10 in) food box with its metal
handles and fittings, to the collapsible food bag which looks
like an ordinary shoulder bag but is lined with insulating fibre.

All the containers work on the same principle: a chemical
which works to keep the container's contents cool is put inside
the receptacle with the food. The chemical can either be of the

*Available from camp site shops

use-once-and-throw-away variety, or it can be the type that is reused after refreezing (larger sites offer facilities for refreezing sachets in their freezers). Using ice-cubes instead of the chemical product is not very satisfactory as the cubes start to melt the moment they are taken out of the freezer, but they can be used in emergency. Cool boxes work well if they are packed with food that is already frozen or very cold, and they will keep the temperature low for twelve hours. If, however, you only put a few lukewarm items in, the low temperature may only last for six hours or so.

Specialised insulated items include ice buckets, ice bowls and butter dishes. They are all useful but it must be said that there is no substitute for a proper refrigerator. It is, of course, a matter of personal preference but we would always choose a conventional caravan refrigerator in preference to a camping box, if only because it does not have to be carried around.

Watch your weight
There is one vital point to be borne in mind as you install your cooking appliances and refrigerator. *You must watch your van's weight.* Your trailer without any optional extras is in its unladen weight form. The weight that should concern you as you start to load the van is its 'maximum gross weight' (mgw). Put simply, this is the weight that the chassis is designed to carry. Every manufacturer quotes an mgw figure for his trailer and this is the figure that must not be exceeded when you set off on tour. A typical tourer has a loading margin between its unladen weight and its mgw of some 150–200 kg (3–4 cwt). This may sound a lot, but just two gas containers add up to 25 kg ($\frac{1}{2}$ cwt). Add an oven and another 13·6 kg (30 lb) or so has gone without even considering the weight of the refrigerator. And there are personal possessions to be considered as well as accessories such as barbecues. It is very easy to overload a trailer and it is also possible to overload a motorcaravan, a fact not often realised by motorcaravanners. Loaded weight can be checked at the nearest weighbridge. A phone call to the nearest council office will direct you to it.

If, after checking your laden weight, you find that you are near the maximum, or even over it, you could change from four-ply to six-ply tyres, as this will increase the mgw, but it is a matter that should be discussed with your caravan dealer. And remember, the mgw of a trailer caravan should not be increased to the point at which it exceeds the towcar's kerbside weight (the weight of the car without driver or passengers but with a full supply of fuel, water, tools and other equipment with which the car is supplied). If your caravan is heavier than your towcar, the car will have great difficulty in pulling the heavy van and, on top of this, you will not be able to travel at 50 mph under the 1973 Motor Vehicles (Variation of Speed Limits) Regulations. You will have to stick to 40 mph – if you can. So do not install too many appliances without checking their weight, unless you're looking for a new and bigger car!

Water supply

If there is one area in which motorcaravans score over trailers, it is in the provision of water for the van. The former have large water tanks under the body of the vehicle and these can be filled in minutes with a hose; the trailer caravanner has to collect his water and bring it back to the van in some kind of carrying receptacle. There are probably as many water carriers on the market as there are caravanners to use them, but the most popular seem to be ordinary jerricans and the Aquaroll water carrier. The latter is a 27-litre (6-gallon) plastic container 46 cm (18 in) long, which comes complete with a filling funnel tube and a detachable handle. Once you have rolled the water back to the trailer, the container stands on its end and is used as a water tank either in or underneath the caravan. You can also buy collapsible trolleys to wheel around jerricans, and polythene water-storage tanks which can be big enough to hold 70 litres (15 gallons). The few tanks which can be built into trailers carry a weight penalty and so are not really advisable, unless you have some spare weight to be used up.

Once you have safely delivered the water to the trailer door there remains the problem of how to get it to the van sink. Trailers at the budget end of the market do not have a foot pump as standard, though they normally offer a foot or hand pump as an optional extra. If you are not going to take up the option you will have to buy a water carrier with a pouring lip so that you can direct water into the sink or pots and pans. However, we suspect that anyone who first decides not to have a pump will soon change his mind. Imagine washing vegetables or meat or doing the washing up without tap water! There are two types of pump on the market, manual and electric, together with many faucets. Assuming you only want to pump cold water from a jerrican to the sink, practically any electric or manual pump will do the job, but if you want to install a water heater – yet another sophistication – it may be worthwhile to pick your water heater first and then find a compatible pump.

Water heaters
Choice of heater is determined by what you want and the available space in the trailer. Some smaller heaters will not operate more than one outlet; if you want a supply of hot water to the toilet room as well as the kitchen sink, you will have to buy one of the larger models. There are several British manufacturers of caravan heaters so you should be able to find the model that particularly appeals to you. However, bear in mind when making your choice of heater and pump that having a high-output pump that fills a kettle in seconds may be satisfying but it is emptying your water container at the same rate. Unless you have a willing band of water carriers or

actually enjoy wheeling water from the site tap to your van, pick a pump with a less forceful output, bearing in mind the requirements of any water heater. A slower stream of water out of the faucet will mean that you are less likely to overfill kettles, pots and pans, and so will become water-conscious.

Sooner or later you will find algae – a green or brown plant growth – in your water containers and lengths of hose. A dry container cannot promote the growth of algae, a damp one can, which is why water containers are prone to this, especially if left unused for any length of time. Throw away the hose and replace it with a new one. The quickest way to clean the actual container is to swill it out with a mixture of water and clean, coarse sand, or you can soak the affected surfaces with a solution of one part 20-vol hydrogen peroxide to four parts water (do not let the mixture come into contact with metals). Once the algae have been removed, rinse out with fresh water and then let the container dry with the lid off before you reuse it.

Holiday hygiene

When you pull the plug in your kitchen sink, the water gushes through an outlet underneath the trailer (this applies to motorcaravans as well). It is not very hygienic to let this dirty water go straight on to the grass, and such a practice is banned on many sites. Waste water should be directed into a bucket or some such receptacle. Many caravanners have two Aquarolls or jerricans and use one for fresh, one for waste water. Do label each carrier to prevent mistakes occurring. Most sites have a disposal point for the waste liquid.

One further point in connection with hygiene and water is the latter's purity or otherwise. All caravanners should make sure that the tap they use does, in fact, supply drinking water. This is of paramount importance if touring abroad; hot countries are particularly suspect. Boiling any suspect water for at least five minutes should get rid of most impurities but this is rather a laborious process and expensive on your gas. The alternative is to buy purifying tablets such as Puritabs (from any well-stocked chemist), or to fit a water-filtering unit to your tap. Again, if caravanning abroad remember to wash fruit and vegetables in treated water.

Power supply

If you have fitted an electric pump in the trailer and you have also invested in a cooker hood and a refrigerator which will sometimes run on the 12v supply, and you already have a couple of fluorescent lights, you are asking a lot of your car battery. As caravans get more and more electricity-orientated (not the very cheap vans which do not have an electric circuit), so the loads imposed on the car battery get higher. Without care, your car battery could be flat after a few days of continuous use of van appliances. This is another area where the motorcaravanner scores over the conventional caravanner, for the former probably uses his vehicle for driving every day – and every time he drives off the site, he is recharging his battery. The trailer caravan may be stationary for weeks at a time.

The trailer caravanner should, if he has installed extra electrical appliances, budget for an independent power supply for the van. Buy a second car battery and some kind of receptacle to carry it around in. There are various battery boxes on the market. You will also have to decide whether to install a permanent or portable battery arrangement. The actual cost involved is low but as the subject can be somewhat complicated, you should get advice from a dealer or accessory shop, or, if you are going to fit up the power supply yourself, write to a company such as Lucas or a club such as the Caravan Club asking for further information.

Gas supplies

The power supply which very much concerns the caravan chef is the gas for cooking. The gas used by caravanners is a petroleum by-product stored as a liquid in metal containers. It is often referred to as bottled gas. There are two common forms – Butane and Propane – but most caravanners use Butane rather than Propane. The main supplier in Britain is Calor Gas who supply the Butane in blue containers, the most popular size being the 4·5 kg (10 lb) one. In 1975 Calor launched a new aluminium container which holds more than 6·8 kg (15 lb) of gas; this will probably become the most popular size in years to come. The procedure for buying gas is to pay a deposit on a full container plus the cost of the gas it contains. When the container

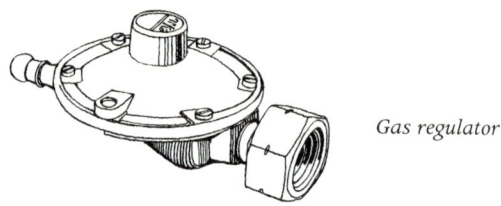

Gas regulator

is empty, it is exchanged for a full one and you only pay for the gas. If you give up the container itself, you receive back the deposit or part of it. The actual price of the gas is about the same as that of household gas if bought in a 4·5 kg (10 lb) container. Many garages and general stores sell Calor Butane gas, as do site shops.

When you buy a container of gas (most caravanners take two with them when touring), you will see a black plastic cap over the outlet nozzle. Make sure that the cap fits snugly and do not take it off until you are ready to use the container. Motorcaravans usually have a ventilated locker for holding gas containers but trailer caravanners keep them outside the van on the drawbar. (When the van is not being used for any period, containers should be stored upright in a safe place away from children, heat and thieves.) There are no vehicle regulations concerning the carriage of gas containers not used for the propulsion of a vehicle, but some tunnels, such as the Mersey Tunnel, do have special conditions. Before using a tunnel check that you can use it while carrying lpg (liquid petroleum gas).

Connecting up the gas supply is simple. The flexible hose which runs from your gas appliances is fitted to the gas container you are going to use by means of a regulator. This device is essential; it slows down the pressure of the gas as it rushes out of the container and makes it acceptable to your appliances. Once the regulator plus hose is on the container, you simply turn on the gas at the container. The cooker is now ready for use. When using the burners you will find them comparable to domestic gas burners, although they are not as effective if there is a draught blowing on them. If the undersides of cooking utensils become 'sooty' there is probably too much air coming through the jets. If you cannot adjust them in accordance with the instructions supplied, call a gas fitter.

The average family uses a pound of gas per day when on tour and one can normally only take three 13·6-kg (30-lb) containers of gas on cross-Channel ferries. Therefore if you are going to be touring abroad for more than a month you will need an alternative gas supply since Calor is not available on the Continent. There are small firms and garages who are willing to refill UK containers but this is prohibited in most countries unless carried out at a designated licensed filling station, so it is unlikely that you will be able to refill Calor containers once you have left Dover. The answer is to switch to Camping Gaz which has outlets all over Europe. The 2·7-kg (6-lb) containers – the most popular size – can be used quite safely as long as you fit an adaptor, obtainable from any Camping Gaz stockist. And if Camping Gaz is not available, you can switch to one of the other bottled gases which are available under various trade names.

Propane gas, mentioned earlier, comes in a red bottle. It is useful in cold climates because it has a lower freezing temperature than Butane and so is less likely to freeze solid in snowy conditions. Caravanners who go skiing in Scotland or one of the European countries where the sport is popular always take Propane in preference to Butane gas. However, the average caravanner who only uses his trailer or motorcaravan in the warm months will never need to switch from Calor Butane unless he is going abroad for a long period, when a switch to Camping Gaz will be necessary anyway.

Gas safety precautions
It cannot be too strongly stressed that gas can be dangerous. Although gas systems rarely go wrong and hundreds of thousands of caravanners use lpg without problems, there are a few simple rules which must be observed. Every time you fit a regulator to a gas bottle, check that the sealing washer is in good repair. Replace it if in doubt. Never tamper with a regulator; if you suspect a fault, take it back to the supplier. At the start of a new caravanning season, bend the hoses and inspect them for cracks. The presence of even a minute crack indicates that the hose should be replaced by another length of lpg hose – not rubber, which is porous. If you think there is a leak somewhere in the gas system, extinguish all naked lights and look for it by rubbing a soapy solution on pipes, joints, etc

as you would look for a puncture in a bicycle tyre. If you do
have a leak you will smell it because the manufacturers add a
'cabbage' smell to the odourless gas as a safety precaution.

When changing containers or fitting regulators you should
not smoke or have any naked flame nearby and you should use
the special spanner supplied for undoing and reconnecting
bottles to regulators (the thread is anti-clockwise). Be sure that
the area is well ventilated. Indeed, adequate ventilation is vital
when any gas-burning appliance is in use: it burns up the
oxygen in the air. If there is no incoming air containing fresh
oxygen your family may fall asleep and be asphyxiated. A
number of deaths occur each year, mainly in immobile vans,
for this reason. Your caravan manufacturer has designed his
van so that there is adequate ventilation. If you 'stop up' any
ventilation vents you are asking for trouble.

Fire drill and prevention

The most dangerous enemy of the caravanner is fire. A trailer
can burn out in four minutes – not a long time to get everyone
out by the limited escape routes available. If your van does
catch alight get everyone out before trying to tackle the blaze;
if necessary, crawl out with your head near the ground where
the air will be more breathable than the smoke-filled upper
parts of the van. If possible, without endangering life, turn off
gas containers and close all doors and windows to help to
contain the fire.

Small fires can be tackled with a fire extinguisher. Although
it is not legally obligatory, every caravan should contain one
and preferably two – one near the door and another near the
cooker. Buy dry powder extinguishers which are BSI (British
Standards Institution) or FOC (Fire Offices Committee)
approved, not the small aerosol type which is inadequate for
anything but the smallest fire and may not work anyway when
you come to use it. Dry powder extinguishers should be used
on fat fires with care as the force with which the foam is ejected
might displace the fat on to the van walls. Use a small asbestos
blanket to smother the blaze or place a lid over the frying pan
to starve the fire of oxygen. Never pour water on a fire caused
by boiling fat as water will spread the blaze, and do not take the
burning pan outside where the wind will fan the flames. A

good preventive measure to take is to flameproof material on all upholstery (and curtains) inside the van; although flame-proofing will not stop the material from catching alight eventually, it will certainly give you time to tackle the fire. You can buy a spray pack for this purpose, one is sufficient for the average caravan.

There are certain obvious precautions to prevent fire, such as being careful with matches. Many caravanners buy a gas lighter which works off a crystal so that they do not have to use naked lights. A fire precaution card for displaying in caravans is available, free of charge, from the Fire Protection Association at Aldermary House, Queen Street, London EC4N 1TJ.

First aid
The one other 'safety' item which every caravanner should carry is a first aid box. Either buy a ready-made kit (from any well-stocked chemist) or you purchase the necessary requisites separately and keep them in a box all together. Make sure that all members of the family know where the box is, but do beware of leaving drugs or sharp implements in accessible places if you have a toddler. Besides any medicines that have been prescribed, we would suggest that your first aid kit contains the following:

cotton wool; lint; plasters and roll of plaster; sterile dressings; rolled elastic and triangular bandages; safety pins; round-edged scissors; eye bath; travel sickness pills; a general antiseptic such as TCP; medicine against upset stomachs; aspirins and water purification tablets; insect repellent; tweezers; and sun-burn cream. It is also a good idea, especially if going abroad, to carry on you a card giving your blood group and details of any allergy.

The most common injuries sustained in caravans are burns and scalds. The immediate remedy for most burns is to plunge the affected part into cold water as soon as possible. Keep the injured part in the water for at least five minutes to cool down the skin. If the burn is really bad the only requisite you need out of your first aid box is dry lint; after the 'water treatment', cover the burn with the lint to keep the injury sterile and go to the nearest hospital or doctor.

Insects

Remember that insects can ruin your holiday and make the cooking a nightmare. Avoid pitching near water as this is where mosquitoes patrol, and do not switch on lights until doors and windows are shut. There are various screens which can be fitted to caravans, but in this country you can probably get by with a packet of Moon Tiger mosquito coils – each coil burns for about seven hours and is harmless to children and pets – or a chemical preparation. Beware of aerosol repellent if spraying near plastic as it may melt it, and do not spray near uncovered food.

Pots and pans

You will need, of course, some pots and pans, a kettle and, if you have an oven, some bakeware. One of the best kettles on the market, which was made for use on Butane gas, is the Squirrel. It is aluminium, has a capacity of four pints and will boil as much as a third faster than ordinary kettles. Normal pots have the disadvantage of being bulky to store but you can get round this problem by buying a packaway set of pans which will also double as cake tins, pudding basins, pie dishes, roasters, etc. There are two sets of Harbenware non-stick Compact Sets – one family size and one slightly smaller – and the pans fit inside each other and are held together by an elastic strap when not in use. The handle is detachable. The Compact Set, which is quite adequate for two, has in it three aluminium pans of 13, 15 and 20 cm (5, 6 and 8 in), three lids and an 18-cm (7-in) frying pan. The family set has two stewpans, 18 and 20 cm (7 and 8 in), two lids, a 15-cm (6-in) milk pan and a 20-cm (8-in) frying pan. There are other makes of nesting pans – most of which do not have the non-stick coating – but Harbenware is the brand leader.

A pressure cooker is a great asset to the caravanner. It cuts down on time and on the amount of Calor gas used. For those who have been wary of using pressure cookers because of the noise they make, there are ranges which have a visual pressure indicator weight and a black central plunger which rises or falls according to the pressure, thus giving more control to prevent hissing. The cookers also have automatic air vents which allow the air to be driven out with the pressure weight already in position, so you do not have to touch the cooker again once it is on the burner. The range includes a 4-litre (7-pint) model ideal for one or two people and a 5·5-litre (10-pint) model suitable for a family.

If you only have two burners the Triple Pan Set sold by Joy & King might appeal to you. The set has three triangular saucepans which fit together so that you can cook three foods at once in the space of one normal pan. Another useful device is the Panfix attachment, a kidney-shaped piece of anodised aluminium which slots over the edge of a frying pan. Cooked fried foods – bacon, sausages, mushrooms, etc – are placed on the attachment to drain and keep hot while you cook more food in the actual frying pan. For families who like to start the day with a pile of toast, the grill can be augmented with one of the many toasters on the market. The most popular is the pyramid shape; it is made of steel, takes up to four slices of toast and fits most burners. The toaster is 16·5 cm (6½ in) square at the base, has a height of 13 cm (5 in) and weighs only 200 g (7 oz). The toast is made by using the heat of one of your burners.

Handy cooking aids

The cooking aids that you pack in the van will depend on the kind of meals that you cook. We would rate as essential a sharp knife which is serrated on one edge for use as a bread knife; a chopping board (which doubles as a bread board) and a small chopping knife for vegetables; a hand whisk; sieve; fish slice and ladle; and a can opener, corkscrew and bottle opener. A handy gadget is a plastic wide-based mixing bowl with a lid which doubles as a grater; you can grate food straight into the bowl and because the lid has holes in it, the whole can be used as a salad shaker or colander. A measuring jug which is marked for foods (flour, sugar, etc) as well as liquid is a boon, as is aluminium foil which can be used for keeping foods hot, separating items while they are cooking, etc, etc. Use of foil will cut down on washing up – use it to line the grill pan to catch fat.

Cutlery

There are various ranges of special caravanning and camping cutlery – some are individual place settings of knife, fork and spoon which clip together to form one unit, others come in plastic wallets – but as a caravanner you do not need these specialised items. Simply buy a cheap set of cutlery (taking the family silver with you is not a good idea as you might lose it) and, if you do not have a built-in segregated cutlery drawer, buy one of these as well. A polystyrene drawer about 37×25 cm $(14\frac{1}{2} \times 10$ in) is quite sufficient and costs only a pound or two. Disposable plastic cutlery saves on washing up, but plastic utensils have a disconcerting habit of breaking and they work out expensive over a period of time.

Crockery

Similarly, disposable crockery – plates and cups – can make a hole in your pocket. However, a supply of paper cups is useful for the breaks en route to the site so that you do not arrive with a sink full of washing up. Apart from this occasional use of paper crockery, it is more economical to buy durable items.

Whether you buy china or plastic crockery is a matter of taste. The ranges of plastic crockery are practically unbreakable, are easy to clean, stack together to save space and come in bright colours, but they do have the disadvantage of becoming stained after some use. (The more expensive brands are less prone to staining than the very cheap.) Many caravanners do not like the feel of them, nor do they like the smell of plastic. Whichever you buy, purchase a crockery rack if you do not have a built-in unit. You can buy a polystyrene rack 48×19 cm $(19 \times 7\frac{1}{2}$ in) which will take cups, saucers and plates; the unit is designed for installation in a cupboard. Alternatively, there are racks which can be attached to walls such as the fold-down plate rack, a chrome-plated storage unit which will take ten full-size plates and only protrudes $2\cdot5$ cm (1 in) when not in use. A similar cup and plate rack will take six cups or beakers and six plates; it measures 33×46 cm $(13 \times 18$ in) and only juts out 8 cm (3 in). The wall racks are better suited to unbreakable crockery since there will probably be some movement of the items when on tow. Whichever crockery you choose, do not forget the glasses and egg cups and, most important, the tea pot and strainer. Buy an insulated teapot to avoid the bother of tea cosies.

Useful oddments

There are one or two other items which you should consider

purchasing. They are all inexpensive, the type of 'odd' accessory which once bought is indispensable. One of these is a purpose-built salt and pepper pot. Made of polythene, it has twin compartments and a three-position stopper which prevents spillage.

A milk-bottle cap combined with a pourer will stop milk spurting out of half-full bottles when the van is being towed. If you are staying on a farm and buying your milk 'straight from the cow' your milk will probably come in a jug which has to be returned to the farmer, so either keep a bottle permanently in the van and decant the jugged milk into it by means of a small funnel, or buy a plastic bottle with a cap which is reserved solely for milk. Similarly, farm eggs are unlikely to be packaged in the usual cardboard boxes; a thin paper bag is nearer the mark! A polythene egg box with six or twelve compartments will store your eggs and protect them when in transit.

Making more space

After storing away all food, cooking utensils, etc and packing the family's personal possessions, you may think that you could do with more storage space. Wait for a while as your packing will certainly improve with practice, but if you still do not have enough space there are various extra units available. Add-A-Drawer is, as its name implies, a drawer which can be fitted in minutes in any space. Made of polystyrene, it measures $28 \times 18 \times 7$ cm ($11 \times 7 \times 2\frac{3}{4}$ in). The Spacesaver Basket $32 \times 24 \times 15$ cm ($12\frac{1}{2} \times 9\frac{1}{2} \times 6$ in) has a slip-on design and provides storage underneath shelves, while a two-tier storage rack can be fitted behind a door or on a wall. Both have a white plastic-coated finish. The similar Multirack fixes against a wall, while polystyrene door liners for bottles and food are attached to the back of a kitchen unit door. There are also larger storage units available which would appeal to the caravanner who doesn't wish to tour around with his caravan but just drives to a site and stays there. One such unit is the Geeco seat which doubles as a storage bin. The hinged lid is shaped and reinforced for seating purposes; the size of the storage bin at its base is 31×21 cm ($12\frac{1}{4} \times 8\frac{1}{4}$ in), height 41 cm ($16\frac{1}{4}$ in). The unit has a handle for carrying. Another more sophisticated storage

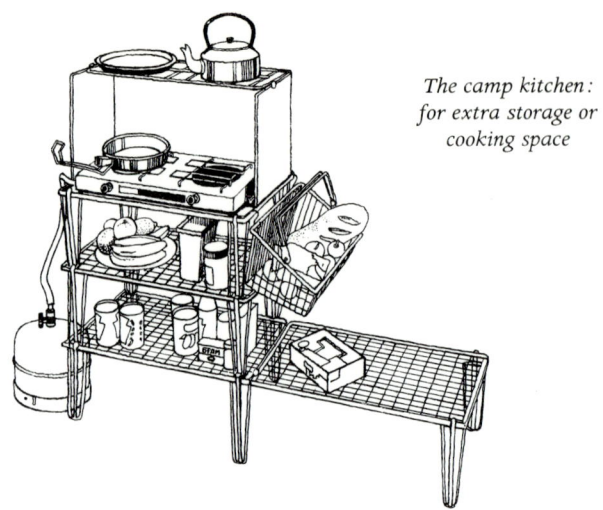

*The camp kitchen:
for extra storage or
cooking space*

item is the camp kitchen which comes in many sizes and folds flat
for transport. Even the smallest has three shelves and a
windbreak; additional shelves and a hanging larder can be
added later. Obviously, the unit cannot be used when you are
towing a trailer or driving a motorcaravan; you have to store it
somewhere when travelling and then erect it, preferably in an
awning, when pitched. Camp kitchens, as the name implies, are
designed to be used as stands for cookers as well as to provide
storage space, but the caravanner can use the shelf intended for
the cooker for food, crockery, etc.

Packing tips
Once you have driven a few hundred miles either pulling a
caravan or driving a motorcaravan, you will discover how
good you are at packing things away by the clutter or lack of it
in the van. As far as possible pack cupboards tightly and fill up
any gaps with polythene bags which will have innumerable uses
on site. If, despite all your efforts you still get irritating rattles
and even breakages, buy a non-stick material to anchor glasses
and breakable items. The non-slip properties are inherent in
the material rather than being achieved with any sticky
adhesive – so there are no cleaning problems. The

20 cm × 2 m (8 in × 6½ ft) reel is ideal for cutting up to use as shelf liners. Available from some chandlers or direct from Dycem Plastics of Parkway Trading Estate, Minto Road, Bristol.

Other 'sticky' things that you will find useful are hooks with self-adhesive backing. If you prefer to keep wet towels outside and also give yourself a drying/airing rack, the hook-on airer gives 6·2 metres (20 ft) of hanging space. It hooks over doors, in and out of windows and can be used single or double. The device folds flat for storage.

Washing up

When washing up in the sink it is most important not to let scraps of food go down the outlet; the plug-hole, like the sink itself, is small and the tiniest scrap will block it. Use kitchen paper to wipe utensils before washing. There are mini washing up bowls available in accessory shops but these are not essential pieces of equipment. What you will find useful is a mini dish-drainer which has been specially designed for small sink units. It measures 30 × 20 cm (12 × 8 in) and takes eight plates and four cups.

On fine days the washing up can be done in a bucket outside the van. Indeed, many caravan chefs also prepare food outside. They take with them a small table and folding chairs so that the table can be used outside the van and the whole ensemble doubles as an outside dining suite. If you want to carry this to sophisticated lengths you can purchase a unit called the Oyster Combi which folds flat for storage. Made from glass fibre with a plastic bowl and steel tubular legs, the Combi is a family-size table; shorten the legs and it is a coffee table; take off the top and it is a sink unit with drainer.

Cleaning up

Finally, the caravan kitchen does score over the domestic variety in the cleaning stakes, simply because there is far less room to keep clean. If the caravan includes a carpet, you could also purchase a mini carpet sweeper which dismantles for storage, but it does seem an unnecessary luxury when there is so little floor area. A triangular dustpan and brush – available from accessory shops – is easy to store. A garbage pail can be unhygienic, and a pedal bin takes up valuable floor space. The

Garbina is very popular; it attaches to a wall or behind a cupboard door and takes plastic throw-away bags.

Of course it is not necessary to buy every gadget and device that has been mentioned. Purchase what suits your family and your cooking as you go along and in the light of your experience. Enjoy your caravanning and enjoy your caravan cooking – the two are not incompatible!

...or do you prefer a tent?

If a caravan seems too sophisticated and expensive to you and all you really want to do is get away from it all and relax, the simple way out is camping under canvas. You can go backpacking, in which case you carry everything with you; you can opt for a small tent from which to make a base for other activities; you can go from point to point by car, using your camping equipment only for sleeping, or, if you go camping *en famille* you can live almost luxuriously in one of those huge canvas bungalows which are so popular today. Your choice of cooking equipment will obviously be geared to the type of camping you do.

Backpacking
For backpacking, everything you need, including the tent, goes into a rucksack on your back so that you are free to walk from place to place, pitching camp when you please. All equipment must be as light as possible so there's no place for heavy saucepans or cookbooks.

Base camping
If you use your tent as a permanent base for such activities as potholing, fellwalking or climbing, then you have a more sophisticated range and choice of equipment. You can also think in terms of a larger stove with perhaps a double burner, or at very least a larger and thus more economical fuel cylinder. If the weather is cold, then you can go for a Propane stove,

since this gas will operate at much lower temperatures than Butane.

Stoves coming in the simple base-camp category are made by Camping Gaz International, Jet Gaz (both French companies and with superb distribution networks), EPIgas, and a new one from Plein Air, not from France as the name suggests, but from Italy. With this type of camping, the cooking is done at the entrance to the tent under the canopy, if you have one, in the open and it is important to see that you select a stove with ample windguards built in.

Gas supplies are something to be considered, too. Once you get away from the weight problem, you can think bigger all round and the bigger the cylinder you can carry, the cheaper will be the cost of the gas in the replacements. In general terms, disposable cylinders are more expensive than the refillable variety. A very popular refillable model is the 907 size from Camping Gaz International. It holds 2·7 kg (6 lb) of liquid gas.

Its greatest asset is its vast replacement network, which extends all over the southern half of Europe. In almost every garage or hardware store you will find the sign displayed. If you reckon on going to the Continent, then this is your best standby cylinder, even if you camp with very sophisticated equipment. It is steady enough on the ground to mount a single

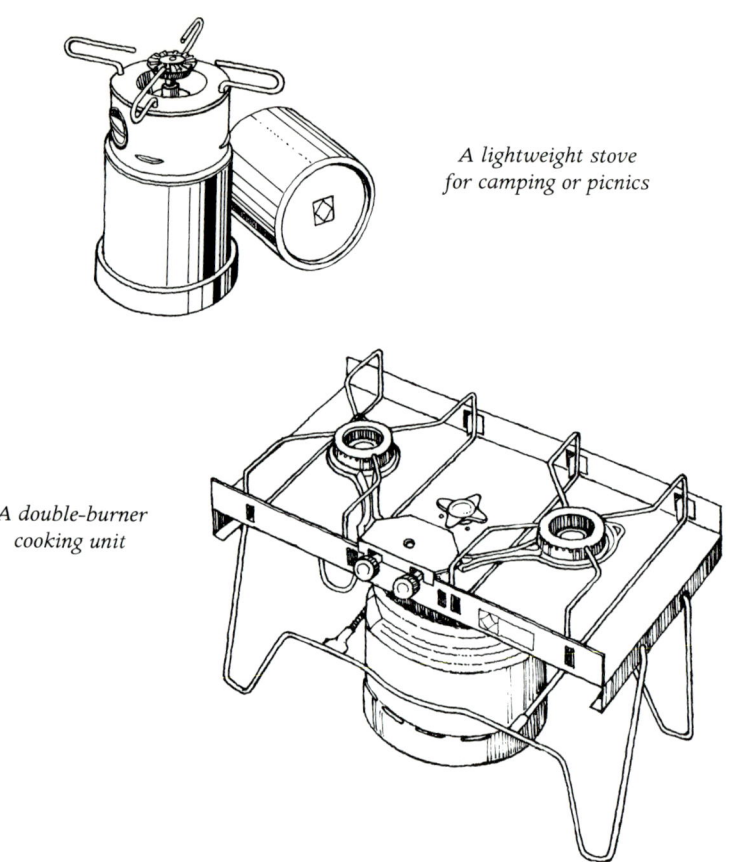

A lightweight stove for camping or picnics

A double-burner cooking unit

burner directly on to it. Lightweight double burners such as the Standard from Camping Gaz are extremely popular, too, as is the Ranch from the same manufacturer.

Cooking pots can be more elaborate than for the backpacker. Nests of saucepans with non-stick inner surfaces are the most practical and several different size packs are made by Harbenware, available from any good camping shop.

Crockery is best in Melamine; it doesn't have to take a lot of knocks in a base camp and should be quite satisfactory. Cutlery can be anything that isn't too precious, but a good stainless steel set will be less likely to suffer from damp and adverse conditions. When it comes to a kettle, there isn't much to touch the Squirrel brand, which has been specially designed to run off low-pressure gas appliances and has a base designed to trap the heat as much as possible. Gas is not cheap and any saving is worthwhile, apart from which the water will heat up more quickly.

Family camping

If you camp with the family and your greatest interest in camping is just to relax on site, then you'll probably pick a location with lots of sunshine and facilities for swimming or boating. This means that you'll erect the tent (or trailer tent) and won't budge until the end of the holiday. So you can go for quite a degree of sophistication in the kitchen. As you have a standing-up space in the tent, the setting-up of tables and chairs and somewhere to put the cooker will present no problems.

There are many special tables for standing the cooker on and there are sophisticated double-burner and grill stoves to enable you to vary the menu. One well-designed unit is the Beanstalk, made entirely in stout wire and clipping together to form a table with shelves underneath, and looking like a set of office trays.

You can of course take as many saucepans as you like, a large frying pan, may be even a pressure cooker. It is possible to take an oven operating from Butane gas. Such items are normally intended to be built into a caravan, but if you have the means of carrying them, what's to stop you making good use of them in your large frame tent? There are camping fridges too, to keep the food fresh in hot weather.

Crockery here can be as lavish as you want to take with you, although some people prefer to use disposable plates and dishes, rather than wash up. But even washing up has been simplified: you can get plastic sink units containing their own water supply and small handpump faucets. Fit one of these into a simple stand and you've really brought the kitchen sink with you.

Barbecues

Barbecuing is now becoming more and more popular for camp cooking. Units come in all shapes and sizes. Very popular with campers these days is the Hibachi range. These barbecues are built in quite heavy cast iron, but are compact and fit readily into the boot of the average car.

The simple portable barbecues, as opposed to the larger type which one would use in the garden, fold away and can weigh as little as 3·2 kg (7 lb). They will grill meat, roast chickens or smoke fish. On some models you can spit-roast chicken and grill steaks at the same time, and some can even be fitted with a power motor. But simple or sophisticated, the basic design is the same: a bowl-shaped tray holds a quantity of charcoal 'briquettes', (small nuggets which are easy and clean to handle) or slabs (both available from hardware stores). Firelighters are a must for best results. The barbecue manufacturers supply specially designed ones which don't taint the food. There are also liquid firelighting products you can use, but never use petrol or paraffin.

You can buy lots of tools and accessories for the job. There are turners, tongs, spoons (for basting), brushes, forks, mitts to protect your hands and bellows to help get the fire going. If you want to protect your clothing there are special aprons you can slip into. They help you look the part at the same time, especially if you happen to be inviting guests from the next tent.

Preparation of the fire is important if you are to achieve good results. In fact it's the be-all and end-all of the situation. To start, first line the tray or bowl of the barbecue with heavy-duty aluminium foil, placing the shiny side uppermost. Pour in a quantity of the charcoal nuggets, spreading them over the entire surface to about 13 mm ($\frac{1}{2}$ in) in depth. (Experience will later tell you exactly how little you can get away with according to the size of the meal you are cooking.) Insert the firelighters and light them.

Now pile the charcoal around the firelighters so that it heats up. Use the bellows freely if you have them, to stimulate the centre of the fire. As it catches, heap more fresh charcoal onto the centre, whilst you spread some of the burning coals out more towards the outer edges. It will take about forty-five minutes to reach the point at which you can begin cooking: you can tell when it is ready by the colour. The centre should be glowing and the charcoal generally should assume a grey tinge.

A family-size tent

Don't now pile fresh fuel on the top, it will only produce more smoke. If the meal is to be a prolonged one, put extra charcoal around the edges, where it can be preheated before actually being used. Only then should it be brought into the centre of the fire. Try to keep the actual cooking area of the fire as flat as possible once the charcoal is well alight: this will ensure that the distance of heat source from the food is fairly even, and so cook the food evenly and avoid burning.

Fat on the outside of joints should be cut away before the cooking is started, otherwise, it will drip on to the fire and produce smoke. Incidentally, take care where you place the barbecue itself, before commencing operations; they tend to smoke and should be sited in a place where not only your own tent but that of your immediate neighbour is not too near. It is important, too, that you choose a position where there is a good chance of air circulating, for the sake of the fire.

Camp fires
This is another method of cooking your meals on site. But here there is a serious snag: in all probability, you won't be allowed to light a fire these days, due to fire risks. This certainly applies to all sites run by the Camping Club of Great Britain and Ireland or the Caravan Club, the two largest organisations in Great Britain. The odd farmer may allow you to build a fire, but

usually only if you are in an organised party or rally. In such cases, it must be built well away from trees or forest terrain. However, if you get the opportunity, here's how to go about it.

First select the spot and if possible, lay back the turf with a spade. It can be replaced afterwards if you don't keep it too near the fire – and only if the ground has cooled sufficiently first. Send the kids out on a wood-hunting spree and segregate their efforts into varying sizes: light brushwood, medium timbers, and heavy pieces. You'll have to come prepared with a saw, to cut some of the larger logs into manageable sizes. If you can find some dead gorse, you'll be able to use it for kindling the smaller brushwood. Once again, firelighters make life easier.

The art of getting a camp fire to burn is to pay attention to how you stack the wood. If you've ever built a house of matches, then you'll understand a little of the technique. The main point to remember is to allow lots of space for the air to circulate – criss-cross the pieces as much as possible, so that they support one another as they burn. Once the centre drops as glowing embers (rather like the charcoal on the barbecue), keeping it alight is much easier, since the intense heat will dry the wood and thoroughly preheat it. For best results in cooking, it is this section of glowing embers which is the part of the fire to use. Like the barbecue, stack the replacement fuel around the edges rather than on top. Do your cooking over the embers and then slowly bring the fresh wood into the fire.

When you have finished, observe a strict safety routine. Remember that a fire started in this way generates an enormous amount of heat: even twelve hours afterwards the ground will probably be unapproachable. A wind springing up overnight can quickly fan it into full blast again and all precautions should be taken to prevent this happening. The best and safest way is to douse it thoroughly with water when you've finished (be careful of the scalding steam as you do it). Make absolutely sure it is quite dead before you leave the field, and if possible, replace the turf you removed before you started the fire. Remember too, that the wind direction can change during the night. The fire you lit downwind could very well be in direct line with your tent if the wind veers round – so don't take any chances by leaving it partly alight when you go to bed. (See

also the section on fire drill on page 24 of the Caravanning
Section.)

CARAVANNER'S CHECKLIST

Cleaning and washing
brush and pan
bucket
clothes airer and/or
  hanging gadgets
detergent
dish drainer
dish mop
disposable cloths
floor cloth
garbage pail
kitchen paper
toilet paper
pot scourer
rubbish bags
tea towels
washing up bowl
washing up liquid
waste water
  container(s)
water container(s)
  and trolley

Cooking appliances and accessories
barbecue and fuel
camping stove
food flasks
gas containers
gas hose (spare)
gas regulator
gas spanner
portable oven
toaster

Cooling appliances and accessories
camping box
cool bags
ice packs
insulated containers
spirit level, levelling
  boards and wheel
  chocks (to ensure
  fridge is level)

Kitchen ware
aluminium foil
bakeware
bottle opener
board for chopping/
  bread
can opener
colander
corkscrew
condiment set
crockery
cutlery
egg boxes
egg cups
fish slice
food – basic and
  emergency
glasses
kettle
kitchen tools
knives
measuring jug
milk container,
  cap and pourer
mixing bowl
potato peeler
pots and pans
pressure cooker
scissors
sieve
tea pot
tea strainer
whisk

Outdoor accessories
chairs
table

Safety and hygiene/ medical equipment
ashtrays
fire extinguisher(s)
first aid kit
insect repellent
hydrogen peroxide
lighter
Milton
smothering cloth
water purifier

Storage
adhesive tape
bags
camp kitchen and
    other storage
    units

rubber bands
square containers
    with lids

Miscellaneous
rubber mat

shopping bag
spare battery
table cloth/mats
clothes and other
    personal
    belongings

CAMPER'S CHECKLIST

barbecue equip-
    ment (see
    Caravanner's
    checklist)
bottle opener
can opener
chairs or stools
chopping board
clothing
corkscrew
cups and saucers
    (or mugs) and
    plates
cutlery
dish mop
disposable cloths
drying up cloth
first aid kit
foodstuffs

frying pan
gas cylinders (full)
heater
insecticides
insect repellent
kettle
mallet
matches
packet foods and
    other provisions
personal
    belongings
plastic bowl
potato peeler
puncture outfit for
    airbeds
repair kit for
    canvas
salt and pepper

saucepans
scissors
scourers
seam wax
silicone spray
    (aerosol)
stove
string
tables
tumblers
washing powder
washing up liquid
waste bin or sack
waste water
    container
water carriers

USEFUL ADDRESSES

ACP CARAVAN AND CAMPING ACCESSORIES Sedgeley Park Industrial Estate, George Street, off Bury New Road, Prestwich, Manchester M25 8WD

BINLEYS CAMPING CENTRE Victoria Street, Kettering, Northants

JOY & KING LTD 15 Alperton Lane, Perivale, Greenford, Middlesex

LUCAS ELECTRICAL LTD Parts and Service Division, Great Hampton Street, Birmingham B18 6AU

THE CARAVAN CLUB East Grinstead House, East Grinstead, West Sussex RH19 1UA

THE CAMPING CLUB OF GREAT BRITAIN AND IRELAND 11 Lower Grosvenor Place, London SW1W 0EY

ROYAL AUTOMOBILE CLUB PO Box 100, Lansdowne Road, Croydon CR9 2JA

GOOD HOUSEKEEPING INSTITUTE, Chestergate House, Vauxhall Bridge Road, London SW1V 1HF

The recipes

It is perfectly possible to serve mouth-watering meals in a caravan. All it needs (as it does at home, for that matter) is a little forward planning and method. And there are great advantages to cooking in the country, where most caravanners make for during the touring season. Food bought in country towns or villages is often cheaper and fresher than food in the cities. At certain times of the year, in fact, it's not just cheap— it's actually free! On one camping site we know there are pounds of blackberries to be picked from hedges literally alongside the van; small wild trout are easily caught from the site itself; and less than a mile away you can spin for mackerel and be assured of a basketful with just a few casts.

But not all sites are so bountiful and the recipes in this book have been created bearing in mind all the different places you may choose to spend your holidays. First, there's the farm – where you may be able to buy relatively cheap fresh dairy products – cheese, milk, cream, eggs and home-grown vegetables; then the country caravan parks – with small shops where fresh food is generally rather expensive but packets and cans are plentiful; there are seaside parks – again with camp site shops but also, hopefully, lots of locally caught fish for sale on the quayside; finally, imagine a sylvan setting, miles from anywhere with the birds and butterflies for company but only your storecupboard to rely on for the main ingredients to prepare your meal.

The storecupboard

If you use your caravan regularly for weekends as well as annual holidays, keep a basic storecupboard in the caravan of dry and long lasting ingredients packed in suitable easy-to-store containers. A basic storecupboard might include:
salt, pepper and other seasonings
granulated and brown sugar
coffee, tea and teabags

dried milk for use in emergencies
instant potato
herbs and spices, for example, dried mixed herbs, curry
powder, paprika, dried parsley, cinnamon
a 'Jif' lemon
ready-mixed French dressing
dried packet vegetables, soups and sauces
a few emergency cans of baked beans, etc

The oven
Don't assume your holiday cooker will react in the same way as
your cooker back home: be prepared for a little trial and error.
The cooker we used to test these recipes (a Flavel cooker using
Calor gas) had two burners, a grill and an oven. We found that
the two burners reacted much as you'd expect; the grill used a
lot of fuel and was not as hot as a normal gas grill; the oven had
settings, $\frac{1}{4}$, $\frac{1}{2}$, $\frac{3}{4}$ or full flame control but it was difficult to assess
the actual temperature of these settings at any given time and
of course, if the burners or grill are used at the same time as the
oven, the oven temperature will drop: be sure to read the
manufacturer's instructions carefully and use your own eye
and judgement.

A typical caravan cooker, with grill and oven

Cook's tips

Cans are a vital part of holiday cooking, but go easy on storing up before you go because they are heavy and take up valuable space and most camp sites have a wide range to choose from.

Buy square rather than round plastic or polythene containers – they fit together snugly without wasting space.

Either store packets of dried foods in a large container or keep them together with elastic bands.

Decant the contents of glass jars into plastic or polythene containers – not only saves space, but weight too and avoids spills.

Keep all food in one storage unit as far as possible.

Store salt and pepper in mills or drums to prevent spilling and breakage.

Take a good supply of stock cubes, chicken and beef and use wherever stock is required or a dish lacks flavour.

Milk powder, reconstituted following the manufacturer's instructions, is ideal for use in sauces, batters and custards – and of course saves carrying heavy milk bottles.

Sauce mixes, for example, white, parsley, onion and cheese are quick to make and add flavour and variety to all sorts of dishes.

Cans of condensed soup turn simple foods into instant casseroles. Simply pour the undiluted soup over fried liver, meat or fish, etc and reheat.

Canned vegetables add variety to the menu if fresh produce is not easily available. Particularly versatile are: tomatoes, baked beans, sweetcorn, mushrooms, red kidney beans and peas.

If you are relying completely on the storecupboard use canned fish or meat to make an appetising meal: tuna, prawns or shrimps, sardines or herrings, chopped ham and pork, ham or corned beef.

Top ice cream with bottled sauces, a can of fruit or a fruit pie filling to ring the changes on a favourite holiday pud.

Instant potato is a real cheat but a great help for ultra-quick meals. Flavour well with butter, seasoning and perhaps cheese.

Potato pancakes

450 g (1 lb) potatoes, peeled
50 g (2 oz) butter or margarine
30 ml (2 level tbsp) flour
2 eggs
milk to mix
salt and freshly ground pepper
oil or fat for frying

Coarsely grate the potatoes into a bowl. In another bowl soften the fat if necessary, beat together with the flour and eggs. Add the egg mixture to the potatoes with enough milk to make a thick batter. Season well. Heat the fat in a frying pan, add spoonfuls of the mixture and cook, turning once, until brown on both sides, about 15 minutes. Drain.
Serving suggestion: fried eggs and bacon.

Danish egg and bacon cake

6 rashers of bacon, derinded
6 large eggs
568 ml (1 pint) milk
salt and freshly ground black pepper

Fry the bacon in its own fat until crisp. Remove from the frying pan. Retain enough bacon fat to grease the pan lightly. Beat the eggs thoroughly, add the milk and seasoning. Reheat the bacon fat and add the egg mixture. Cook over a low heat until the eggs begin to set, shaking the pan from time to time. Arrange the bacon rashers like spokes of a wheel over the egg mixture and continue cooking until the mixture has set. Serve straight from the pan.
Serving suggestion: grilled or fried tomatoes and crusty fresh bread.

Spanish potato omelette

50 g (2 oz) butter
2–3 potatoes, peeled and cooked
4 eggs
50 g (2 oz) cheese, grated or cut into small cubes
salt and pepper

Melt the butter in a frying pan. Chop or slice the cooked potatoes and fry until golden. Beat the eggs, cheese and seasoning together, add to the pan and cook over a gentle heat, tilting the pan to allow the uncooked egg to run to the sides until golden underneath and set on the top. Serve immediately.
Serving suggestion: grilled bacon and tomatoes.

Sausages in bacon

225 g (8 oz) chipolata sausages
French mustard
8 rashers of streaky bacon, derinded
566-g (20-oz) can of baked beans

Grill the sausages under a hot grill until evenly browned, about 10 minutes. Remove from the pan, spread with a little mustard and wrap each sausage in a rasher of bacon. Return to the grill pan and cook until the bacon is crisp, turning occasionally. Heat the beans in a saucepan. Serve the beans topped with the sausages.

Cheese scramble

3–4 eggs, beaten
30 ml (2 tbsp) cream or top of milk
salt and pepper
5 ml (1 level tsp) mustard
75 g (3 oz) butter or margarine
50 g (2 oz) cheese, grated or cut into small cubes
4 slices of bread

Beat the eggs, milk, seasoning and mustard together. Melt 25 g

(1 oz) of the fat in a saucepan, add the egg mixture and cook over a low heat, stirring until the mixture begins to set. Stir in the cheese. Remove the pan from the heat and continue stirring until the cheese melts. Toast the bread and spread with the remaining butter or margarine. Pile the scramble on top of the toast and serve immediately.

Scrambled eggs with bacon and rice

4 rashers of streaky bacon, derinded
60 ml (4 tbsp) milk
75 g (3 oz) cooked long grain rice
4 eggs, beaten
salt and pepper
4 slices of bread
50 g (2 oz) butter or margarine

Chop the bacon finely and fry in a saucepan until crisp. Add the milk, rice, eggs and seasoning. Cook gently, stirring continuously, until the mixture sets lightly. Meanwhile toast the bread and butter well. Pile the egg mixture on to the toast and serve immediately.

Mushrooms and bacon on toast

4 slices of bread
50 g (2 oz) butter or margarine
225 g (8 oz) mushrooms, sliced
2 rashers of bacon, derinded and chopped
salt and pepper

Try this made with field mushrooms (see page 148), if you are lucky enough to find them. Field mushrooms usually need wiping to remove the dirt and, unless they are *very* small, it is best to remove their rather tough skins.

Toast the bread on both sides and butter well. Melt the remaining fat in a saucepan, add the sliced mushrooms and bacon and cook until the bacon is crisp. Pile on top of the toast and serve immediately.

Kippers and mushrooms on toast

75 g (3 oz) butter or margarine
325 g (12 oz) kipper fillets
100 g (4 oz) mushrooms, halved
4 slices of wholemeal bread
lemon juice
salt and freshly ground pepper

Melt half the fat in a frying pan, add the kipper fillets and cook for 2 minutes on each side. Push to one side of the pan, add the mushrooms and cook until tender, about 5 minutes. Toast the bread and butter. Pile the mushrooms on the toast and top with the kipper fillets. Sprinkle with lemon juice and seasoning.

Creamed haddock

325–450 g (12 oz–1 lb) smoked haddock
300 ml ($\frac{1}{2}$ pint) milk
1 packet of white sauce mix
100 g (4 oz) cheese, grated or cut into small cubes
salt and pepper

Wash and trim the fish and place in a saucepan with the milk, reserving 45 ml (3 tbsp) milk. Bring to the boil, cover and simmer gently for 10–15 minutes, until tender. Remove the fish from the pan, skin and flake. Blend the sauce mix with remaining cold milk, add to the fish liquor and continue to make up the sauce as directed on the packet. Add the cheese and stir until it melts. Add the flaked fish and seasoning and heat through.
Serving suggestion: hot buttered toast.

Kedgeree

325 g (12 oz) smoked haddock
175 g (6 oz) long grain rice
75 g (3 oz) butter
2 hardboiled eggs, shelled and chopped
salt and freshly ground pepper

Kedgeree

Wash and trim the fish, put in a pan, cover with water and bring to the boil. Remove from the heat, cover the pan and leave to stand for 5–10 minutes, until the fish is tender. Drain, skin and flake the fish. Cook the rice in boiling, salted water for 10–15 minutes, until tender. Drain. Melt the butter in a pan, add the fish, rice, eggs and seasoning; stir over a gentle heat until thoroughly heated through, about 5 minutes. Serve immediately.

Cod's roe en croûte

50 g (2 oz) butter or margarine
4 slices of white bread
325 g (12 oz) cooked cod's roe
30 ml (2 level tbsp) flour
salt and freshly ground pepper
8 rashers of streaky bacon, derinded
2 tomatoes, halved

Melt the fat in a frying pan, add the bread and cook until

golden brown on both sides; remove from the pan. Coat the cod's roe in seasoned flour, add to the pan and cook each side for about 5 minutes. Push to one side of the pan, add the bacon and tomatoes and cook until the bacon is crisp. Place cod's roe on bread and serve with bacon and tomato.

Swiss apple muesli

60 ml (4 tbsp) rolled oats or fine oatmeal
150 ml ($\frac{1}{4}$ pint) fruit juice
4 eating apples
60 ml (4 tbsp) cream or top of milk
15 ml (1 tbsp) honey
15 ml (1 level tbsp) brown sugar
50 g (2 oz) sultanas or raisins
50 g (2 oz) chopped nuts – hazelnuts, walnuts, almonds

Place the oats and fruit juice in a bowl and leave overnight. In the morning, grate or chop the apples into the bowl and add the remaining ingredients. Divide between serving dishes. Serve sprinkled with a few nuts.

Swiss apple muesli

♨ ♨ Cauliflower and bacon soup

1 small cauliflower
50 g (2 oz) butter or margarine
1 onion, skinned and chopped
1 carrot, scraped and chopped
900 ml (1½ pints) chicken stock
salt and pepper
4 rashers of streaky bacon, derinded

Break the cauliflower into small florets. Melt the fat in a large saucepan, add the cauliflower, onion and carrot and cook for 5 minutes. Stir in the stock and seasoning, bring to the boil, cover and simmer gently for 20 minutes. Chop the bacon into small pieces and cook in its own fat until crisp. Drain and stir into the soup.
Serving suggestion: crusty rolls.

♨ Kidney and celery broth

225 g (8 oz) ox kidney
30 ml (2 tbsp) vegetable oil
2–3 sticks of celery, washed and finely sliced
1 medium onion, skinned and finely chopped
900 ml (1½ pints) beef stock
salt and pepper
50 g (2 oz) long grain rice (optional)

Cut the kidney into bite-size pieces, removing all the core. Heat the oil in a large pan, add the kidney and brown evenly, about 5 minutes. Remove from the pan and reserve. Add the vegetables and cook over a low heat until soft, about 5 minutes. Return the kidney to the pan with the stock, seasoning and rice, bring to the boil and simmer gently for 20–25 minutes, until the kidney is tender.
Serving suggestion: crusty bread or wholemeal toast.

♨ Cheddar cheese soup

25 g (1 oz) butter or margarine
1 large onion, skinned and chopped
30 ml (2 level tbsp) flour
10 ml (2 level tsp) dry mustard
600 ml (1 pint) chicken stock
300 ml ($\frac{1}{2}$ pint) milk
175 g (6 oz) Cheddar cheese, grated or cut into small cubes
salt and pepper

Melt the fat in a saucepan, add the chopped onion and cook gently until soft, about 5 minutes. Stir in the flour and mustard. Add the stock, milk and cheese. Cook over a gentle heat, stirring occasionally, until the cheese has melted and the soup comes to the boil. Season to taste.
Serving suggestion: crusty rolls or bread.

♨ ♨ Celery and mushroom soup

425-g (15-oz) can of cream of celery soup
425-g (15-oz) can of cream of mushroom soup
25 g (1 oz) butter or margarine
50 g (2 oz) button mushrooms, sliced
60 ml (4 tbsp) top of the milk or cream

Heat the celery and mushroom soup together in a saucepan without boiling. Melt the fat in a separate pan, add the mushrooms and cook until lightly browned. Serve the soup with the milk or cream swirled over the top and sprinkled with mushrooms.

♨ Quick tomato soup

556-g (20-oz) can of tomato juice
63-g (2$\frac{1}{4}$-oz) can of tomato purée
150 ml ($\frac{1}{4}$ pint) chicken stock
5 ml (1 level tsp) salt
5 ml (1 level tsp) sugar
pepper

Place all the ingredients together in a large saucepan. Bring to the boil and simmer gently for 5–10 minutes.
Serving suggestion: crusty bread or bacon flavoured crackers.

Haddock chowder

25 g (1 oz) butter or margarine
1 onion, skinned and sliced
2 rashers of bacon, derinded and chopped
3 potatoes, peeled
225 g (8 oz) haddock, skinned
425-g (15-oz) can of tomatoes
600 ml (1 pint) chicken stock
salt and pepper

Melt the fat in a large saucepan, add the onion and bacon and cook for 5 minutes. Cut the potato and the fish into 1-cm ($\frac{1}{2}$ -in) cubes. Add to the pan with the tomatoes, stock and seasoning. Bring to the boil, cover and simmer gently for 25–30 minutes, until the fish is tender.

Cheese and apple rarebit

1 medium cooking apple
50 g (2 oz) butter or margarine
100 g (4 oz) cheese, grated or cut into small cubes
pinch of dry mustard
salt and freshly ground pepper
30 ml (2 level tbsp) cornflour
4 rashers of lean bacon, derinded
4 slices of bread

Peel, core and finely chop the apple. Melt half the fat in a pan add the apple and cook until soft but not pulpy, about 5 minutes. Add the cheese, mustard, seasoning and cornflour and continue cooking, stirring continuously until the cheese melts and the mixture thickens. Grill the bacon and toast the bread under a hot grill. Butter the toast, spoon the apple mixture on to it. Return to the grill and cook until the mixture browns. Top with the bacon. Serve immediately.

Golden corn

4 slices of bread
50 g (2 oz) butter or margarine
4 eggs
60 ml (4 tbsp) cream or top of milk
salt and pepper
198-g (7-oz) can of sweetcorn, drained

Toast the bread and butter well. Beat the eggs, cream and seasoning together. Melt the remaining fat in a saucepan, add eggs and corn and cook over a low heat, stirring, until the eggs begin to set. Pile on to the toast and serve immediately.

Tomato and cheese rarebit

25 g (1 oz) butter or margarine
45 ml (3 level tbsp) flour
226-g (8-oz) can of tomatoes
5 ml (1 level tsp) mustard
salt and pepper
175 g (6 oz) cheese, grated or cut into small cubes
8 slices of white bread

Melt the fat in a saucepan, stir in the flour and cook for 2 minutes without browning. Add the tomatoes and cook until the mixture thickens. Stir in the mustard, seasoning and cheese. Heat the mixture until the cheese melts, stirring. Toast the bread on one side, spread the untoasted side with the tomato and cheese mixture. Brown under the grill.

Eggs benedict

4 slices of bread
4 slices of ham
1 packet of white sauce mix
300 ml ($\frac{1}{2}$ pint) milk
75 g (3 oz) cheese, grated or cut into small cubes
salt and pepper
4 eggs

*A variety of
toasted snacks*

Toast the bread on one side, place the ham on the untoasted side and grill slowly to heat through. Make up the white sauce following the instructions on the packet. Stir in the cheese, season to taste. Poach the eggs, place on top of the ham and coat with cheese sauce.

Swiss toast

4 slices of bread
50 g (2 oz) butter or margarine
30 ml (2 level tbsp) chutney
4 slices of luncheon meat
4 slices of cheese
2 tomatoes, sliced

Toast the bread, butter the untoasted side and spread with chutney. Top with the luncheon meat and cheese and grill until the cheese begins to melt. Top with the tomato slices and continue grilling until the tomato is cooked.

Ham and cheese deckers

8 slices of bread
100 g (4 oz) butter or margarine
4 slices of ham
mustard
4 slices of cheese
2 tomatoes, sliced
salt and pepper
Worcestershire sauce

Toast four slices of the bread on both sides and butter well. Arrange a slice of ham on each and spread with mustard. Grill to heat the ham. Toast the remaining four slices of bread on one side. Spread the untoasted sides with butter, top each with a slice of cheese, decorate with tomato slices and sprinkle with seasoning and Worcestershire sauce. Place under the grill and cook until the cheese bubbles. Place one slice of cheese toast on top of each of ham toasts and serve immediately.

To make this snack more substantial top with another slice of buttered toast.

Ham and cheese deckers

Tomato and egg savoury

425-g (15-oz) can of tomatoes
1 clove of garlic, skinned and crushed (optional)
45 ml (3 tbsp) vegetable oil
3 eggs, beaten
salt and pepper
4 slices of hot buttered toast

Simmer together tomatoes, garlic and oil until the mixture thickens. Add the eggs and seasoning and cook gently until eggs are set. Pile on to hot buttered toast.

Cheese and onion crisp

2 large onions, skinned and sliced
4 slices of bread
50 g (2 oz) butter or margarine
100 g (4 oz) Cheddar cheese
salt and pepper

Cook the onion in boiling salted water for 5–10 minutes, drain well. Toast the bread under a heated grill. Butter the toast, cover with onion slices and crumble cheese over the top. Season well. Return to the grill and cook until the cheese melts and bubbles. Serve immediately.

Open sandwiches

For a quick, attractive snack, open sandwiches are ideal, using different combinations of ingredients you already have at hand. For the 'base' use pumpernickel, rye, brown, white or crisp bread; rolls cut into three, horizontally; crackers or French bread. Whichever base you choose butter it thickly before adding the 'top'. Here are some suggestions:
Lettuce, flaked salmon mixed with mayonnaise, decorated with sliced cucumber.
Hardboiled eggs and shrimps, topped with mayonnaise.
Cottage cheese mixed with diced pineapple, decorated with watercress.

Sliced cheese, sliced tomato, anchovy fillets and black olives.
Sliced ham, coleslaw, tomato slices.
Sliced tongue, cream cheese, stuffed olives.
Lettuce, pâté, sliced tomato.
Sardine in tomato sauce and watercress.
Sliced liver sausage, sliced tomato, watercress.
Lettuce, pâté, horseradish cream.

♨ Quick shrimp risotto

100 g (4 oz) long grain rice
25 g (1 oz) butter or margarine
1 small onion, skinned and chopped
2·5–5 ml ($\frac{1}{2}$–1 tsp) curry powder
1 small apple, cored and chopped
226-g (8-oz) can of tomatoes
5 ml (1 tsp) chutney (optional)
100 g (4 oz) peeled shrimps, fresh, frozen or canned
salt and freshly ground pepper

Cook the rice in boiling salted water for 10–12 minutes, until
just tender. Drain. Melt the fat in a frying pan, add the onion
and cook until golden brown, about 5 minutes. Add the curry

*Quick
shrimp
risotto*

powder and apple and cook for 1 minute more. Add the rice, tomatoes, chutney and shrimps to the curry mixture and thoroughly heat through. Season and serve immediately.

♨ Rice cakes

6 rashers of bacon, derinded
175 g (6 oz) cooked long grain rice
3 eggs, beaten
salt and pepper
butter or margarine

This is an ideal way of using up leftover cooked long grain rice.

Chop the bacon and fry it in its own fat until crisp. Drain and mix with the rice, eggs and seasoning. Heat a little fat in a frying pan and drop in spoonfuls of the mixture. Cook the cakes on one side until golden, turn and cook other side. Serve while very hot.

Serving suggestion: fried tomatoes.

♨ ♨ Special savoury macaroni

50 g (2 oz) butter or margarine
1 medium onion, skinned and chopped
4 rashers of streaky bacon, derinded and chopped
4 tomatoes, chopped
175–225 g (6–8 oz) quick-cook macaroni
100 g (4 oz) cheese, grated or cut into small cubes
Worcestershire sauce
salt and pepper

Melt the fat in a frying pan, add the onion and cook until soft, about 5 minutes. Add the bacon and continue cooking until the bacon is crisp. Add the tomatoes and cook until tender. Meanwhile cook the macaroni in boiling, salted water for 7–10 minutes, until tender. Drain well and stir in the cheese, Worcestershire sauce and seasoning. Reheat to melt the cheese if necessary. Stir the bacon mixture into the macaroni and serve immediately.

Pan pizza

90 ml (6 level tbsp) flour
pinch of salt
45 ml (3 tbsp) vegetable oil
226-g (8-oz) can of tomatoes, drained
2·5 ml ($\frac{1}{2}$ level tsp) mixed herbs
75–100 g (3–4 oz) cheese, sliced
60-g (2-oz) can of anchovy fillets or sardines, drained
  (optional)
black olives (optional)

Make the Pan pizza with all its topping ingredients for special occasions. The simpler version without anchovies and olives makes an equally filling, tasty snack.

    Stir the flour and salt together in bowl. Add 15 ml (1 tbsp) oil and enough water to mix to a soft dough. Knead gently. Roll or press out dough so that it will fit the base of a large frying pan. Heat the remaining oil in the frying pan and fry until golden, about 5 minutes. Turn the dough over and, while the second side is cooking, spread the tomatoes over the cooked side and

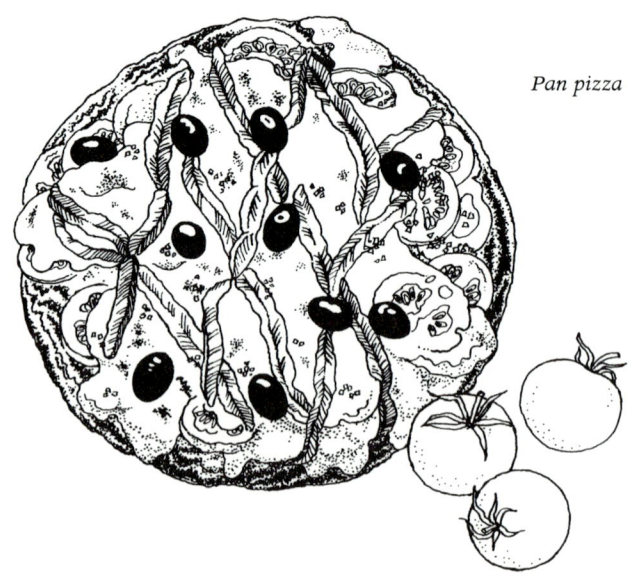

Pan pizza

sprinkle it with herbs. Top the pizza with cheese slices, anchovies or sardines and black olives. When the second side is golden brown, place the whole pizza under a hot grill and cook until the cheese melts and bubbles.
Serves 2–3

Seafood omelette

4 eggs
salt and pepper
25 g (1 oz) butter
1 packet of white sauce mix
300 ml (½ pint) milk
100 g (4 oz) peeled prawns, fresh, canned or frozen

Beat the eggs and seasoning together. Melt the butter in an omelette or frying pan, add the eggs and cook over a low heat, gently stirring, until set. Make up the sauce following the instructions on the packet. Add prawns and seasoning and heat through. Serve the omelette with sauce poured over it.
Serves 2

Smoked haddock omelette

100 g (4 oz) smoked haddock, cooked
50 g (2 oz) butter
142-ml (5-fl oz) carton of double cream
3 eggs, separated
30 ml (2 level tbsp) grated Parmesan cheese
salt and pepper

Flake the fish, removing any skin and bones. Melt half the butter in a saucepan, remove from the heat, add fish and 45 ml (3 level tbsp) cream. Stir in the egg yolks, half the cheese, season to taste. Whisk the egg whites until stiff and fold into the fish mixture. Melt the remaining butter in a frying or omelette pan, pour in the mixture and cook until the underside is golden brown. Blend the remaining cheese and cream together, pour over the omelette and cook under a hot grill until the cheese mixture melts and bubbles.

Serving suggestion: French bread and green salad.

Serves 2

Sausage and sweet pepper omelette

50 g (2 oz) butter
225 g (8 oz) chipolata sausages
1 small green pepper, seeded and finely sliced
a small bunch of spring onions, trimmed and sliced
3 eggs
30 ml (2 tbsp) milk
salt and pepper

Melt half the butter in frying pan and cook the sausages until golden all over, about 10 minutes. Remove from the pan and cut each sausage into four. Wipe out the pan with a paper towel. Add the remaining butter and sauté the vegetables for 5–10 minutes. Beat the eggs, milk and seasoning together and

Sausage and sweet pepper omelette

pour into the pan over the vegetables. Add the sausages and cook until the egg mixture is set. Serve at once.
Serves 2

Broccoli ham rolls

225 g (8 oz) broccoli
4 slices of ham
1 packet of white sauce mix
300 ml ($\frac{1}{2}$ pint) milk
75 g (3 oz) cheese, grated or cut into small cubes
salt and pepper

We have used broccoli to fill the ham rolls, but you might like to try another vegetable, such as chicory or celery.

Cook the broccoli in boiling salted water for 10 minutes, drain; divide the florets between the ham slices and roll up. Place in an ovenproof dish. Make up the white sauce following the instructions on the packet. Add half the cheese and stir until melted. Pour the cheese sauce over the ham rolls and sprinkle the remaining cheese on top. Cook under a hot grill for 10–15 minutes, until the cheese melts and begins to bubble.

Pork potato cakes

198-g (7-oz) can of chopped ham and pork
30 ml (2 level tbsp) instant potato powder
1·25 ml ($\frac{1}{4}$ level tsp) dry mustard
salt and pepper
milk
15 ml (1 level tbsp) flour
cooking oil or fat

Chop the meat finely. Heat 90 ml (6 tbsp) water in a pan to boiling point, add to the instant potato and mix well. Add the meat, mustard, seasoning and a little cold milk to bind if necessary. Divide the mixture into four, shape into cakes and coat in seasoned flour. Heat the fat in a frying pan and cook the cakes for 5–10 minutes each side until golden brown.
Serving suggestion: baked beans and fried tomatoes.

Pork and mushroom sauté

450 g (1 lb) pork sausagemeat
salt and freshly ground pepper
30 ml (2 level tbsp) flour
25 g (1 oz) lard
100 g (4 oz) streaky bacon, derinded and chopped
50 g (2 oz) button mushrooms, sliced
283-g (10-oz) can of condensed mushroom soup

Divide the sausagemeat into sixteen balls and coat in seasoned flour. Heat the lard in a frying pan and cook the balls with the bacon and mushrooms until golden brown, 10–15 minutes. Drain off excess fat. Stir in the soup and heat through, stirring.
Serving suggestion: crusty bread, rolls or toast.

Ham roll ups

100 g (4 oz) cooked long grain rice
2 hardboiled eggs, chopped
45 ml (3 tbsp) bottled mayonnaise
2–3 gherkins, chopped (optional)
salt and pepper
4 slices of cooked ham

Mix together the rice, eggs, mayonnaise and gherkins, season well. Divide the mixture between the ham slices and roll each slice up tightly.
Serving suggestion: tomato and cucumber salad and crusty rolls.

Celery au gratin

1 head of celery
1 packet of white sauce mix
300 ml ($\frac{1}{2}$ pint) milk
100 g (4 oz) cheese, grated or cut into small cubes
salt and pepper

Also try this recipe using 2–3 hardboiled eggs and cooked cauliflower instead of celery.

Wash the celery and cut into 2·5-cm (1-in) lengths. Cook in

Ham roll ups

boiling, salted water for 10–15 minutes, until tender but still crisp. Drain well. Make up the white sauce, following the instructions on the packet. Add half the cheese and stir until it melts. Add seasoning. Place the celery in an ovenproof dish, pour the sauce over it, sprinkle with the remaining cheese. Cook under a hot grill until the cheese melts and bubbles. *Serving suggestion:* hot buttered toast or crusty rolls.

Spicy tomato grill

25 g (1 oz) butter or margarine
1 small onion, skinned and finely chopped
226-g (8-oz) can of tomatoes
2·5 ml ($\frac{1}{2}$ level tsp) mixed herbs
5 ml (1 tsp) Worcestershire sauce
salt and freshly ground pepper
50–100 g (2–4 oz) lean ham
2 hardboiled eggs
100 g (4 oz) Cheddar cheese, grated or sliced

Melt the fat in a saucepan, add the onion and cook until soft, about 5 minutes. Add the tomatoes, herbs, Worcestershire sauce and seasoning. Bring to the boil and simmer gently for about 10 minutes to reduce and thicken the liquid. Cut the ham into thin strips and add to the tomato mixture. Cut the eggs in half lengthways, place cut side down in an ovenproof dish. Pour tomato mixture over them and top with cheese. Cook under a hot grill until cheese melts and bubbles.

Beef 'n' banger burgers

225 g (8 oz) minced beef
225 g (8 oz) sausagemeat
salt and freshly ground pepper
a little flour
4 crusty rolls or baps
4 lettuce leaves, washed (optional)
60 ml (4 level tbsp) chutney
1 small onion, skinned and thinly sliced

Stir mince, sausagemeat and seasoning together until well blended. Divide the mixture into four and with floured hands shape into burgers. Place the burgers under a heated grill and cook for 5–10 minutes on each side. Split rolls or baps and place a lettuce leaf on the base of each. Top each with a burger, chutney and onion. Serve immediately.

Beef 'n' banger burgers

*Liver skewers
with scrambled eggs*

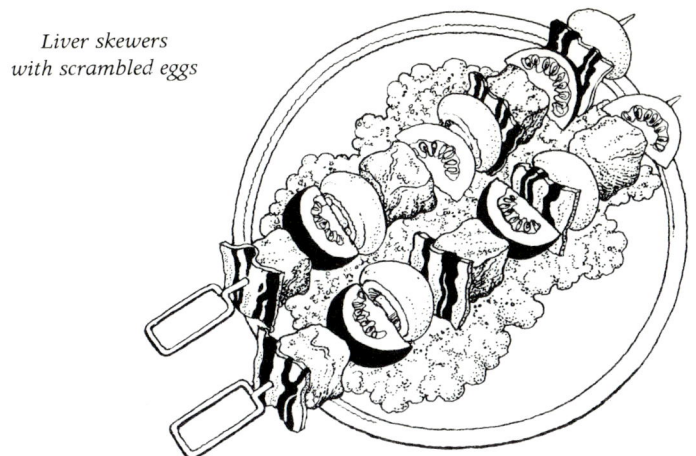

Liver skewers with scrambled eggs

325 g (12 oz) lamb, chicken or pig's liver
4 rashers of streaky bacon, derinded
4 tomatoes, quartered
100 g (4 oz) mushrooms, fresh or canned
melted butter
salt and pepper
6 eggs
60 ml (4 tbsp) cream or top of the milk

If you haven't got skewers, pick four straight greensticks and remove the bark.

Wash and dry the liver and cut into 2·5-cm (1-in) cubes. Cut bacon into 2·5-cm (1-in) pieces. Arrange the liver, bacon, tomatoes and mushrooms on four skewers. Brush with melted butter, season and cook under a hot grill for 10–15 minutes, turning each skewer twice and brushing on more butter each time. Beat eggs, season and cream together. Heat 25 g (1 oz) butter in pan, add eggs and cook over a low heat, stirring, until mixture thickens. Pile scrambled eggs on plates and top with skewers.

Serving suggestion: French bread and butter or hot buttered toast.

Potato pan fry

60 ml (4 tbsp) vegetable oil
1 large onion, skinned and chopped
225 g (8 oz) lean bacon, derinded and chopped
450 g (1 lb) cooked potato, chopped
salt and freshly ground pepper
4 eggs (optional)

To make a more filling meal, top with fried eggs.

Heat the oil in a large frying pan, add the onion and bacon and cook until the onion is soft, about 5 minutes. Push to one side of the pan. Fry the potato in the same fat until golden brown on all sides. Remove from the pan and toss well with seasoning. Fry the eggs until the white is set and serve on top of the potato mixture.

Ham and egg savoury

1 small green pepper, seeded and chopped (optional)
50 g (2 oz) butter or margarine
30 ml (2 level tbsp) flour
150 ml ($\frac{1}{4}$ pint) milk
170-g (6-oz) can of condensed chicken soup
100 g (4 oz) ham, chopped
3 hardboiled eggs, chopped
2·5 ml ($\frac{1}{2}$ level tsp) salt
pepper
4 slices of bread

Put the green pepper in a saucepan, cover with cold water, bring to the boil and simmer for 5 minutes; drain. Melt half the fat in a pan, stir in the flour and cook for 1–2 minutes. Remove the pan from the heat, gradually stir in milk. Return the pan to the heat, bring to the boil and cook for 1–2 minutes. Stir in the soup, green pepper, ham, eggs and seasoning and heat through, stirring occasionally. Toast the bread and spread with the remaining butter. Pile the mixture on to the toast and serve immediately.

Main meals for high days and holidays

Fisherman fricassée

1 packet of cheese sauce mix
1 packet of parsley sauce mix
568 ml (1 pint) milk
198-g (7-oz) can of tuna, drained
326-g (11½-oz) can of sweetcorn, drained
50 g (2 oz) cheese, grated or cut into small cubes

A tasty meal from your storecupboard.

Blend together the sauce mixes in a saucepan. Stir in the milk and make up the sauces following the instructions on the packet. Flake the tuna, add to the sauce with the sweetcorn and heat thoroughly, stirring occasionally. Pour the mixture into an ovenproof dish, sprinkle with cheese and brown under a hot grill.

Herrings in cider

4 herrings
25 g (1 oz) butter
1 medium onion, skinned and chopped
2 eating apples
300 ml (½ pint) cider
10 ml (2 level tsp) cornflour

Wash the herrings, remove fins, heads and tails, remove backbone if you wish (see page 146). Melt the butter in a frying pan, add the onion and cook until soft, about 5 minutes. Core and slice the apples into wedges, add with the cider to the pan and bring to the boil. Add the fish to the pan and simmer gently for 10 minutes. Turn and cook the second side for 10 minutes. Place the herrings on a hot plate and cover. In a small bowl, blend the cornflour to a smooth paste with a little water. Add the cornflour to the pan, stirring continuously, bring back to

Herrings in cider

the boil and cook until the sauce thickens. Spoon the sauce over the herrings and serve.

Serving suggestion: endive and celery salad.

Tuna Manitoba

½ large cucumber
50 g (2 oz) butter or margarine
100 g (4 oz) button mushrooms
283-g (10-oz) can of condensed mushroom soup
198-g (7-oz) can of tuna, drained
salt and pepper
3 tomatoes, quartered

Cut the cucumber into thick slices. Melt the fat in a saucepan and cook the cucumber and mushrooms until tender, about 5 minutes. Add the soup to the pan with the tuna and seasoning and heat through gently. Garnish with tomato wedges.

Serving suggestion: boiled rice or ribbon pasta.

Cod sauté

4 rashers of streaky bacon, derinded
1 medium onion, skinned and thinly sliced
340-g (12-oz) can of potatoes, drained and cubed
5 ml (1 level tsp) paprika (optional)
300 ml ($\frac{1}{2}$ pint) chicken stock
4 tomatoes, skinned
450 g (1 lb) cod fillet, skinned
10 ml (2 level tsp) cornflour
5 ml (1 level tsp) tomato purée
salt and pepper
142-g (5-fl oz) carton of soured cream or top of the milk
   (optional)

A really tasty complete meal cooked in just 30 minutes. You can use fresh potatoes instead of canned but if so, cook them until tender before adding to the dish.

Chop the bacon and fry in its own fat in a saucepan with the onion until it begins to colour, about 5 minutes. Add the potatoes, paprika and stock. Bring to the boil, cover and simmer for 10 minutes. Cut the tomatoes into wedges and the fish into chunks. Add to the pan, cover and simmer gently for 10–15 minutes. Blend the cornflour to a smooth paste with a little water and add to the pan with the tomato purée and seasoning, stirring all the time. Bring back to the boil and simmer until the sauce thickens. Stir in the soured cream.

Serving suggestion: green salad.

Spiced cod au gratin

4 cod steaks, fresh or frozen
25 g (1 oz) butter or margarine
30 ml (2 level tbsp) tomato chutney
50–75 g (2–3 oz) Cheddar cheese, sliced
4 tomatoes, halved

Place the cod steaks on a grill pan, dot with fat and cook under a hot grill for 5–10 minutes. Turn, dot with more fat and cook for 5 minutes more. Spoon chutney on to each steak and top

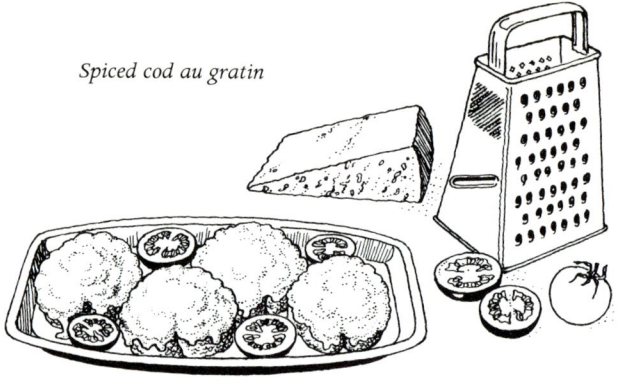

Spiced cod au gratin

with sliced cheese. Add the tomatoes to the grill pan, return to the heat and grill until the cheese is golden and bubbling. *Serving suggestion:* potato crisps and a green salad.

♨ Chicken salad with rice

100 g (4 oz) long grain rice
450 g (1 lb) cooked chicken
2 red eating apples
lemon juice
1 medium cauliflower, cut into florets
1 green pepper, seeded and finely sliced
142-ml (5-fl oz) carton of soured cream or natural yoghurt
1 small lettuce, washed

For the dressing
90 ml (6 tbsp) vegetable oil
60 ml (4 tbsp) vinegar
pinch of dry mustard (optional)
pinch of paprika (optional)
salt and freshly ground black pepper

Cook the rice in boiling salted water for 12–15 minutes. Drain. Make up a salad dressing by shaking the ingredients together in a lidded container. Pour half over the rice and leave until completely cold. Cut the chicken into strips. Core and cube the apples and dip immediately in lemon juice. In a bowl combine the cauliflower, pepper, apple and remaining salad dressing. Stir in the soured cream or yoghurt, chicken and rice. Serve on a bed of lettuce.

Curried potato and frankfurter salad

two 210-g (7½-oz) packets of frankfurters or 450 g (1 lb) cooked
  chipolata sausages
822-g (1-lb 12 oz) can of potatoes, drained or 450 g (1 lb)
  cooked potatoes
226-g (8-oz) jar of mayonnaise
10 ml (2 tsp) lemon juice
10 ml (2 level tsp) concentrated curry sauce or curry powder
2 sticks of celery, washed and chopped
2–3 spring onions, skinned and chopped
1 Cos or Webb's lettuce

Cook the frankfurters in boiling water for 5 minutes, drain and cool. Slice each sausage diagonally into four and chop corner

Chicken salad with rice

ends. Cut the potatoes into large dice. Turn the mayonnaise into a bowl, stir in the lemon juice and curry. Add the potatoes, celery and onions, stir until well coated. Arrange the lettuce on four serving plates. Pile potato mixture in the centre of each plate and arrange frankfurters on top.

Serving suggestion: crusty rolls or French bread.

♨ Salad niçoise

226-g (8-oz) packet of frozen whole green beans
226-g (8-oz) can of tuna fish
½ cucumber, thinly sliced
4 tomatoes, quartered
10–12 black olives
60-g (2-oz) can of anchovy fillets or sardines, drained

For the dressing
90 ml (6 level tbsp) bottled mayonnaise
60 ml (4 tbsp) olive or vegetable oil
30 ml (2 tbsp) wine vinegar
2·5 ml (½ level tsp) salt
freshly ground black pepper

Cook the beans in boiling salted water for 4–5 minutes; drain and cool. Flake the fish. Place the beans and fish together in a large bowl. Make up the dressing by shaking the ingredients together in a lidded container. Pour the dressing over the bean mixture and gently toss. Arrange cucumber slices around the edge of four serving plates. Pile bean mixture in the centre of each plate. Garnish with tomato wedges, black olives and anchovies.

Serving suggestion: crusty French bread or rolls and butter.

Mexican bean salad

425-g (15-oz) can of red kidney beans
4 sticks of celery, washed and chopped
4–6 gherkins, chopped (optional)
1 medium onion, skinned and finely chopped
175 g (6 oz) cooked ham, beef or other cold meat
1 Cos or Webb's lettuce
4 hardboiled eggs, sliced

For the dressing
60 ml (4 tbsp) olive or vegetable oil
30 ml (2 tbsp) vinegar
2·5 ml ($\frac{1}{2}$ level tsp) French mustard
pinch of sugar
salt and freshly ground black pepper

Drain the kidney beans and combine in a bowl with the celery,

*Mexican
bean salad*

gherkins and onion. Place the dressing ingredients in a lidded container and shake well. Pour the dressing over the bean mixture and stir. Cut the meat into strips and stir in with the beans. Arrange the lettuce leaves on four serving plates, pile mixture in the centre of each plate, garnish with egg slices.
Serving suggestion: crusty French bread or rolls and butter.

Crispy salad with zesty dressing

1 large onion, skinned
4 sticks of celery, washed
$\frac{1}{2}$ cucumber
100 g (4 oz) Edam or Cheddar cheese
225 g (8 oz) ham, salami or cooked meat
1 small curly endive or lettuce

For the dressing
90 ml (6 level tbsp) bottled mayonnaise
60 ml (4 level tbsp) horseradish sauce
10 ml (2 level tsp) French mustard
5 ml (1 tsp) vinegar
salt and pepper

Slice the onion thinly, chop the celery, cut the cucumber into strips, cut the cheese into matchstick lengths, cut the meat into strips. Stir the dressing ingredients together in a bowl. Season well. Coat the onion, celery, cucumber, cheese and meat thoroughly in dressing. Wash the endive or lettuce and arrange on a plate, top with the dressed salad.
Serving suggestion: fresh rolls or French bread and butter.

Pork fricassée

450 g (1 lb) pork sausagemeat
100 g (4 oz) streaky bacon, derinded and chopped
1 packet of parsley sauce mix
300 ml ($\frac{1}{2}$ pint) milk
226-g (8-oz) can of butter beans, drained
50 g (2 oz) Cheddar cheese, grated or cut into small cubes

Divide the sausagemeat and shape into sixteen balls. Fry with the bacon until the sausagemeat is golden and the bacon crisp, about 10–15 minutes. Drain off excess fat. Make up the parsley sauce following the instructions on the packet. Add the sausagemeat balls, bacon and butter beans to the sauce and heat through gently. Turn the mixture into an ovenproof dish, top with cheese and cook under a hot grill until the cheese melts and bubbles.

Serving suggestion: crisp green salad and crusty bread.

Caravanner's mixed grill

4 lamb cutlets
salt and pepper
2 tomatoes, halved
4 large mushrooms
225 g (8 oz) chipolata sausages
4 rashers of bacon, derinded
melted butter or vegetable oil

Trim the chops and season well. Arrange the tomatoes and mushrooms in the base of the grill pan, where they will be basted by the juices from the food above. Place the grill grid in the pan, arrange the chops, sausages and bacon on top, brush with the fat and cook under a hot grill, turning frequently, until evenly browned, about 15–20 minutes.

Serving suggestion: green salad.

Chipolata special

100 g (4 oz) noodles
15 ml (1 tbsp) vegetable oil
225 g (8 oz) chipolata sausages
226-g (8-oz) can of tomatoes
1 small clove of garlic, crushed
salt and pepper
2·5 ml ($\frac{1}{2}$ level tsp) sugar

Cook the noodles in boiling, salted water for 8–10 minutes until tender; drain. Heat the oil in a frying pan and cook the sausages until evenly brown, about 10 minutes. Push to one side of the pan, add the tomatoes, garlic, seasoning and sugar. Simmer for 5–10 minutes, mashing the tomatoes with a spoon. Serve the noodles with sausages and sauce.

Sausages with barbecue sauce

450 g (1 lb) pork sausages
175 g (6 oz) pasta shells
knob of butter
freshly ground black pepper

For the sauce
50 g (2 oz) butter or margarine
1 medium onion, skinned and chopped
226-g (8-oz) can of tomatoes
10 ml (2 level tsp) tomato purée
30 ml (2 tbsp) vinegar
30 ml (2 level tbsp) demerara sugar
10 ml (2 level tsp) mustard
30 ml (2 tbsp) Worcestershire sauce

To make the sauce, melt the fat in a saucepan, add the onion and cook until soft, about 5 minutes. Add the remaining sauce ingredients, cover and simmer for 25 minutes. Grill the sausages until browned on all sides, 10–15 minutes. Cook the pasta in boiling salted water for 15 minutes. Drain, add a knob of butter and season with pepper. Divide the pasta between four plates, place sausages on top and pour barbecue sauce over. *Serving suggestion:* green salad.

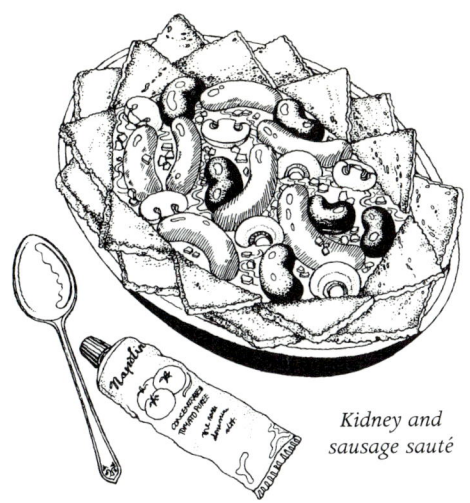

*Kidney and
sausage sauté*

♨ Kidney and sausage sauté

10 lambs' kidneys
50 g (2 oz) butter or margarine
225 g (8 oz) chipolata sausages
1 large onion, skinned and chopped
100 g (4 oz) button mushrooms, halved
15 ml (1 level tbsp) tomato purée
300 ml ($\frac{1}{2}$ pint) beef stock
salt and freshly ground pepper
15 ml (1 level tbsp) cornflour

Skin the kidneys, cut in half lengthways and core. Heat the fat in a frying pan, add the sausages and cook until brown all over. Push to one side of pan, add the onion and mushrooms and cook for 5 minutes more. Add the kidneys and cook over a gentle heat for 5 minutes until evenly coloured. Stir in the tomato purée, stock and seasoning. Bring to the boil and simmer gently, stirring occasionally, for 15–20 minutes. Blend the cornflour with a little water, add to the pan and continue cooking until the sauce thickens.
Serving suggestion: boiled rice or toast triangles.

Mexican style frankfurters

25 g (1 oz) butter or margarine
1 large onion, skinned and chopped
5–10 ml (1–2 tsp) chilli seasoning
425-g (15-oz) can of tomatoes
210-g (7½-oz) can of red kidney beans, drained
226-g (8-oz) can of frankfurter sausages, drained and thickly
    sliced
salt and freshly ground black pepper
8 slices of French bread
100 g (4 oz) Cheddar cheese, sliced

Melt the fat in a frying pan, add the onion and cook until soft, about 5 minutes. Add the chilli seasoning and cook for 1 minute, stirring. Add the tomatoes, beans, sausages and seasoning. Bring to the boil, stirring, and simmer for 10–15 minutes. Meanwhile toast the bread on one side, place the cheese slices on the untoasted side and grill until golden and bubbling. Spoon frankfurter mixture on to four serving plates and serve with two slices of French bread each.

Liver in savoury cream sauce

25 g (1 oz) butter or margarine
1 medium onion, skinned and sliced
225 g (8 oz) courgettes, trimmed and sliced
450 g (1 lb) lamb's liver
salt and pepper
10 ml (2 level tsp) flour
150 ml (¼ pint) chicken stock
15 ml (1 tbsp) lemon juice
2·5 ml (½ level tsp) marjoram
142-ml (5-fl oz) carton of single cream or top of the milk

Melt half the fat in a frying pan and sauté the onion until soft, about 5 minutes. Add the courgettes and cook for a further 5 minutes. Push to one side of the pan. Cut the liver into cubes, coat in seasoned flour. Add the remaining fat to the pan and cook the liver until browned all over. Add stock, lemon juice and marjoram; season to taste. Bring to the boil and simmer gently for 5 minutes. Stir in the cream and reheat but do not boil.

Serving suggestion: green salad.

♨ Liver stroganoff

50 g (2 oz) butter or margarine
1 large onion, skinned and chopped
100 g (4 oz) mushrooms, sliced
30 ml (2 level tbsp) flour
salt and pepper
450 g (1 lb) lamb's liver, cut into strips
283-g (10-oz) can of condensed mushroom soup
cream or top of the milk (optional)

Melt the fat in a frying pan, add the onion and mushrooms and cook until the onion is soft, about 5 minutes. Meanwhile put the flour, seasoning and liver strips in a plastic bag, hold the top and shake the bag to coat the strips in flour. Push the onions and mushrooms to one side of the pan, add the liver and cook until browned all over. Stir in the soup, bring to the boil, stirring. Cover and simmer gently for 10–15 minutes. Stir in the cream and serve.

Serving suggestion: boiled rice or pasta shells.

♨ ♨ Curried eggs

6 eggs
15 ml (1 tbsp) vegetable oil
2 medium onions, skinned and chopped
15 ml (1 level tbsp) curry powder
5 ml (1 level tsp) curry paste (optional)
5 ml (1 level tsp) tomato purée
30 ml (2 level tbsp) flour
400 ml ($\frac{3}{4}$ pint) chicken stock
1 medium cooking apple, peeled, cored and chopped
225 g (8 oz) long grain rice

Boil the eggs for 8 minutes. Heat the oil in a saucepan, add the onion and cook until soft, about 5 minutes. Stir in the curry powder, curry paste, tomato purée and flour and cook over a low heat for 2–3 minutes, stirring continuously. Gradually stir in the stock and apple, bring to the boil and simmer gently for about 15 minutes, stirring occasionally. Meanwhile cook the rice in boiling salted water for 12–15 minutes, until tender. Drain the rice and divide between four plates. Shell the eggs and cut in half lengthways. Arrange them in the centre of the plates and top with curry sauce.

Serving suggestion: mango chutney, tomato and onion salad.

♨ Quick savoury mince

15 ml (1 tbsp) vegetable oil
1 onion, skinned and chopped
2–3 large carrots, scraped and chopped
450 g (1 lb) minced beef
298-g (10½-oz) can of oxtail soup
salt and pepper
100 g (4 oz) peas, fresh, frozen or canned (optional)

Heat the oil in a frying pan, add the onion and carrots and cook until the onion is soft, about 5 minutes. Add the mince and cook until browned. Stir in the soup and seasoning. Bring to the boil, cover and simmer gently for 20–30 minutes until the meat is tender. Stir in the peas and heat through.

Serving suggestion: potatoes, rice or crusty French bread.

♨ Quick steak diane

50 g (2 oz) butter
1 small onion, skinned and finely chopped
salt and pepper
4 thin (minute) steaks
30 ml (2 tbsp) Worcestershire sauce
15 ml (1 tbsp) lemon juice
10 ml (2 tsp) chopped parsley (optional)

Heat the butter in a frying pan, add onion and cook until soft,

Quick steak diane

about 5 minutes. Push to one side of the pan. Season the steaks, add to the frying pan and cook for 1 minute on each side. Push the steaks to one side of the pan. Add the Worcestershire sauce and lemon juice to the pan juices, blend together and heat through. Add parsley and cook gently for 1 minute. Serve the steaks with sauce poured over them.
Serving suggestion: mixed salad and crusty bread or crisps.

♨ Beefburgers with mushroom sauce

25 g (1 oz) butter or margarine
1 large onion, skinned and chopped
100 g (4 oz) mushrooms, sliced
8 beefburgers, fresh or frozen
salt and pepper
283-g (10-oz) can of condensed mushroom soup

You'll find this a tasty way to dress up beefburgers and a recipe that will be a favourite when you get home.

Melt the fat in a frying pan, add the onion and cook until soft, about 5 minutes. Add the mushrooms and continue cooking for 2 minutes. Push to one side of the pan. Fry the beefburgers until browned on both sides, remove from the pan and keep warm. Add seasoning and soup and heat gently, stirring. Serve beefburgers with sauce poured over them.
Serving suggestion: pasta, rice or crisps and a salad or green vegetable.

♨ Italian style beefburgers

25 g (1 oz) butter or margarine
8 beefburgers, fresh or frozen
1 medium onion, skinned and chopped
1 clove of garlic, skinned and crushed
3 large tomatoes, chopped or a 226-g (8-oz) can of tomatoes
150 ml ($\frac{1}{4}$ pint) beef stock
30 ml (2 level tbsp) tomato purée
1·25 ml ($\frac{1}{4}$ level tsp) Italian seasoning or mixed herbs
salt and pepper

Melt the fat in a frying pan, add the beefburgers and fry until brown on both sides. Remove from the pan and cut each into four strips. Add the onion and crushed garlic to the pan and cook until the onion is soft, about 5 minutes. Return the beefburgers to the pan with the remaining ingredients and simmer uncovered for 5–10 minutes.
Serving suggestion: instant or canned potatoes or freshly cooked pasta.

♨ Savoury fried chicken

4 chicken joints
1 egg
half 99-g (3-oz) packet of sage and onion stuffing
salt and pepper
60 ml (4 tbsp) vegetable oil
1 lemon, quartered

Skin the chicken joints, cut each in half. Beat the egg in a shallow bowl or dish. Mix the stuffing and seasoning on a plate. Dip the chicken pieces in beaten egg and coat evenly with the stuffing. Heat the fat in a frying pan, add the chicken, cover the pan and cook gently for 10–15 minutes each side, until golden brown. Drain on kitchen paper, serve with lemon wedges.

Serving suggestion: green salad and potato crisps or sticks.

♨ ♨ Chinese style chicken fried rice

100 g (4 oz) long grain rice
4 eggs
salt and pepper
25 g (1 oz) butter
60 ml (4 tbsp) vegetable oil
1 large onion, skinned and chopped
50 g (2 oz) mushrooms, chopped
100-g (4-oz) packet of frozen peas
2 sliced bamboo shoots (optional)
100 g (4 oz) ham, diced
100 g (4 oz) peeled shrimps, fresh, canned or frozen
100 g (4 oz) cooked chicken, chopped
60 ml (4 tbsp) soy sauce

Try your hand at this simple Chinese style dish for a special holiday treat.

Cook the rice in a saucepan of boiling salted water for 12–15 minutes, until tender. Drain. Beat the eggs with 30 ml (2 tbsp) water and seasoning. Melt the butter in a frying pan, pour in the egg mixture and cook as an omelette, until golden brown. Remove from the pan and cut into strips. Heat the oil in the frying pan, add the onion and fry until golden brown, about 10 minutes. Add the rice and heat through. Add the mushrooms, peas, bamboo shoots, ham, shrimps, chicken, and soy sauce. Heat slowly, stirring occasionally until very hot. Divide rice mixture between four plates and top with omelette strips.

♨ ♨ Devilled chicken with rice

25 g (1 oz) butter or margarine
1 large onion, skinned and chopped
25 g (1 oz) flaked almonds
15 ml (1 level tbsp) flour
2·5 ml ($\frac{1}{2}$ level tsp) dry mustard
2·5 ml ($\frac{1}{2}$ level tsp) curry powder
15 ml (1 tbsp) Worcestershire sauce
400 ml ($\frac{3}{4}$ pint) chicken stock
325 g (12 oz) cooked chicken, chopped
salt and pepper
225 g (8 oz) long grain rice

Melt the fat in a saucepan, add the onion and cook until soft, about 5 minutes. Add the almonds and continue cooking until they have browned. Remove the pan from the heat and stir in the flour, mustard, curry powder and Worcestershire sauce. Gradually stir in the chicken stock. Return the pan to the heat and bring to the boil, stirring continuously. Add the chicken and seasoning and simmer gently for about 10–15 minutes. Cook the rice in boiling salted water for 12–15 minutes, until tender. Drain and serve with the devilled chicken.

🗇 Lamb chops with orange salad

4 lamb chops
salt and freshly ground pepper
2 oranges
50 g (2 oz) butter
2·5 ml ($\frac{1}{2}$ level tsp) dried mint or parsley (optional)
$\frac{1}{2}$ cucumber
141-g (5-oz) carton of natural yoghurt
1 small lettuce

Wipe the chops and season well. Place under a hot grill and cook for 10–15 minutes each side. Grate the rind of one orange or peel it thinly and chop finely. Soften the butter if necessary, stir the rind into the butter with mint or parsley and blend well together. Chop the flesh of both oranges, dice the cucumber

and combine with the yoghurt. Wash the lettuce and arrange on a plate; pile orange mixture on top. Serve the chops topped with the orange butter with the orange and cucumber salad.
Serving suggestion: crisps.

Devilled lamb chops

50 g (2 oz) butter
10 ml (2 level tsp) mustard
5 ml (1 level tsp) curry powder
15 ml (1 tbsp) lemon juice
grated rind of $\frac{1}{2}$ lemon
4 lamb chops

Soften the butter if necessary, cream together with the mustard, curry powder, lemon juice and rind. Trim and wipe the lamp chops and place in foil on the grill pan, turn up the edges of the foil to form cups. Spread each chop with the butter, using about half the mixture. Grill for 10–15 minutes, turn and spread the remaining butter on the uncooked side, grill for a further 10–15 minutes. Serve the chops with the devilled butter poured over them.
Serving suggestion: crusty French bread or canned potatoes, heated and tossed in butter, and a green salad.

Grilled gammon with grapes

4 gammon steaks or bacon chops
50 g (2 oz) butter or margarine
30 ml (2 level tbsp) brown sugar
30 ml (2 tbsp) vinegar
100 g (4 oz) grapes, pipped
salt and freshly ground pepper

Cut the rind from the gammon rashers and snip the fat at intervals. Cook under a hot grill for 5–6 minutes each side. Melt the fat in a saucepan add the sugar, vinegar and grapes. Season well and heat gently until the sugar dissolves and the mixture bubbles. Serve the gammon with the sauce.
Serving suggestion: sweetcorn and crisps.

Veal Holstein

25 g (1 oz) butter
4 veal escalopes
salt and pepper
30 ml (2 level tbsp) flour
30 ml (2 tbsp) vegetable oil
4 eggs
60-g (2-oz) can of anchovies, drained
lemon wedges

Melt the butter in a frying pan. Coat the escalopes in seasoned flour, place in the pan and cook for about 5 minutes each side, until golden brown. Push to the side of the pan. Add oil to the pan, break in the eggs, one at a time, and cook until the white is set. Cut the anchovies in half, lengthways. Place an egg on each veal escalope and arrange anchovy fillets over the top in a lattice pattern.

Serving suggestion: green salad and crusty bread or boiled rice.

Veal piquant

50 g (2 oz) butter
salt and pepper
4 veal escalopes
5 ml (1 tsp) vinegar
10 ml (2 level tsp) French mustard
142-ml (5-fl oz) carton of single or soured cream
1 lemon, quartered

This is very simple and quick to prepare – the cream adds a touch of holiday luxury.

Melt the butter in a frying pan. Season the escalopes and place in the pan. Fry for about 5 minutes on each side, until golden brown. Add the vinegar, mustard and cream to the pan, stirring well. Heat gently but do not boil. Serve the escalopes, pour over the sauce and garnish with lemon wedges.

Serving suggestion: peas or green salad, grilled potato croquettes, or crisps.

Quick dishes from the pressure cooker

The pressure cooker is a real boon on a caravanning or camping holiday: with it you can cook satisfying meals quickly and easily without taking hoards of pots and pans. It is especially safe to use in cramped cooking conditions as the hot food is safely sealed inside and cannot be spilt even if the cooker is knocked. By cooking everything in one pan you save fuel too, and the washing up is practically non-existent, particularly if you cook both meat and vegetables together.

To bring the pressure cooker up to the correct pressure follow the manufacturer's instructions. To reduce pressure, use one of the following methods, as indicated in the recipes:

The quick method
Remove the pressure cooker from the heat and place in the sink. Run cold water over the pressure cooker (making sure the water does not run over the weights or the safety plug) *or* stand the pressure cooker in a bowl of cold water. To test if the pressure has reduced, lift the weights slightly: if the cooker hisses, continue running cold water over it. When the pressure is reduced remove the weights and the lid, tilting the lid away from you to ensure the steam escapes away from you. Continue according to the recipe. *Note:* the weights must not be removed until the pressure has been reduced.

The slow method
Turn off the heat or remove the pressure cooker from the hob and leave to stand for about 5 minutes. Remove the weights and lid as above and continue according to the recipe.

Pressure points
Whether you are using the pressure cooker at home or on holiday, there are two important points to remember. First, don't fill the pressure cooker more than two-thirds full: overfilling reduces the space for steam within the pan and may cause the safety valve to blow. Second, always ensure that you

have added a minimum of 300 ml ($\frac{1}{2}$ pint) of liquid, e.g. stock or water, that will turn into steam during cooking. A tip for the holidaymaker: to reduce the pressure quickly, if you stand the cooker in a bowl of cold water you will not only reduce the pressure inside the cooker but heat the washing up water at the same time!

Quick guide to cooking vegetables in the pressure cooker

Vegetable	Method of preparation	Where to cook	Time at high (15 lb) pressure
Beans:			
broad	whole	in separator	4–5 minutes
French	whole or sliced	in separator	4–5 minutes
runner	sliced	in separator	4–5 minutes
Cabbage:			
white, green	shredded	in separator	4 minutes
Carrots	whole, sliced, or cut and diced	in separator	according to size; about 4 minutes
Cauliflower	florets	in separator	4 minutes
	quartered	on trivet	4 minutes
	halved	on trivet	4–5 minutes
Celery	cut into 2·5–5-cm (1–2-in) lengths	in separator	4–5 minutes
Corn on the cob			
small	whole	on trivet	3 minutes
large	whole	on trivet	5 minutes
Marrow	thickly sliced	on trivet	4 minutes
Peas (fresh)		in separator	3 minutes
Potatoes:			
new	whole	on trivet	4–5 minutes according to size;
old	cut	on trivet	4–6 minutes

Pressure cooking pasta and rice

Macaroni, noodles and spaghetti should be cooked in plenty of salted water on their own (there is usually no room to cook the meat at the same time). Use 225 g (8 oz) pasta to 1·1 litre (2 pints) water and cook for 3–6 minutes at high (15 lb) pressure. You can cook long grain rice with the meat by placing the rice in cold salted water in a solid basket or bowl covered with greaseproof paper and standing it in the separator. Use 225 g (8 oz) rice to 600 ml (1 pint) water and cook at high (15 lb) pressure for 5 minutes then reduce the pressure by leaving cooker to cool at room temperature (slow method).

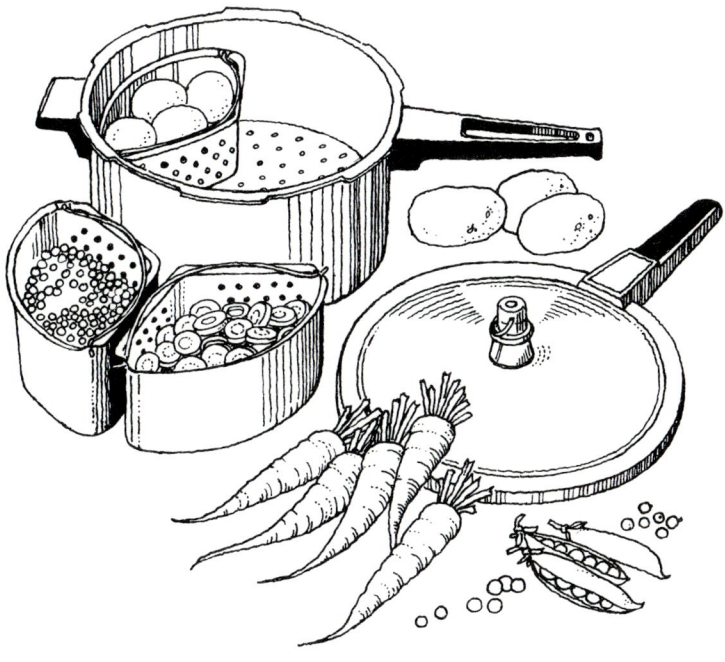

Pressure cooking different vegetables together

Beef and orange casserole

700 g (1½ lb) chuck steak
30 ml (2 tbsp) vegetable oil
1 large onion, skinned and chopped
finely grated rind and juice of 1 orange
300 ml (½ pint) beef stock
2·5 ml (½ level tsp) thyme
salt and freshly ground pepper
15 ml (1 level tbsp) cornflour

Cut the meat into 2·5-cm (1-in) cubes. Heat the oil in the pressure cooker, add the meat cubes and fry quickly until brown all over. Remove the meat. Add the onion and cook until browned, about 5 minutes. Return the meat to the cooker together with the orange rind and juice, stock, thyme and seasoning. Bring to the boil, stirring. Put the lid on the cooker, bring up to high (15 lb) pressure and cook for 20 minutes. Reduce pressure by the quick method. Remove lid. Blend the cornflour with a little water, add to the cooker, stirring and bring back to the boil. Cook until the sauce thickens.

Burgundy beef

30 ml (2 tbsp) vegetable oil
1 large onion, skinned and sliced
1 green pepper, seeded and chopped
700 g (1½ lb) stewing steak
100 g (4 oz) mushrooms, sliced
150 ml (¼ pint) red wine
30 ml (2 level tbsp) tomato purée
salt and pepper

Heat the oil in the pressure cooker, add the onion and pepper and cook until the onion is soft, about 5 minutes. Remove from the cooker and keep on one side. Cut the meat into 2·5-cm (1-in) cubes, add to the cooker and cook until browned all over. Return the onion and pepper to the cooker with the mushrooms, wine, tomato purée and seasoning. Put the lid on the cooker, bring up to high (15 lb) pressure and cook for 20

Burgundy beef

minutes. Reduce pressure by the quick method and serve.
Serving suggestion: freshly boiled rice or buttered new potatoes.

♨ Chilli con carne

15 ml (1 tbsp) vegetable oil
450 g (1 lb) minced beef
1 large onion, skinned and chopped
30 ml (2 level tbsp) tomato purée
10 ml (2 level tsp) chilli seasoning
1 clove of garlic, skinned and crushed
425-g (15-oz) can of tomatoes
150 ml ($\frac{1}{4}$ pint) beef stock
salt and freshly ground pepper
425-g (15-oz) can of red kidney beans, drained or baked beans
15 ml (1 level tbsp) cornflour

Heat the oil in the pressure cooker, add the beef and brown all
over. Add the onion and continue cooking for 2 minutes. Add
the tomato purée, chilli seasoning, garlic, tomatoes, stock and
seasoning and bring to the boil, stirring. Put the lid on the
cooker, bring up to high (15 lb) pressure and cook for 15

minutes. Reduce pressure by the quick method and remove the lid. Add the kidney beans to the cooker and heat through. Blend the cornflour to a smooth paste with a little water, add to the cooker and bring to the boil, stirring. Cook until the mixture thickens.

Serving suggestion: freshly boiled rice.

♨ Meat loaf

325 g (12 oz) minced beef
100 g (4 oz) sausagemeat
2 slices of bread
1 onion, skinned and finely chopped
5 ml (1 level tsp) mixed herbs
15 ml (1 level tbsp) tomato ketchup
15 ml (1 tbsp) Worcestershire sauce
salt and pepper
1 egg, beaten

This is just the thing for a picnic on the beach. Pack it in a sealed container, and prepare a salad to go with it.

Meat loaf

In a mixing bowl, stir the mince and sausagemeat together until well blended. Remove the crusts from the bread, cut the bread into small cubes, add to the bowl with the remaining ingredients and mix well together. Shape into a thick roll that will fit into the pressure cooker. Wrap in double foil, pleating the foil to allow for expansion. Seal each end tightly. Put the trivet in the pressure cooker, place the foil-wrapped loaf on top and add 600 ml (1 pint) hot water. Put the lid on the cooker, bring up to high (15 lb) pressure and cook for 35 minutes. Reduce pressure by leaving the cooker to cool for 5–10 minutes using the slow method. Serve hot or cold.
Serves 4–6

♨ ♨ Spaghetti bolognese

25 g (1 oz) butter or margarine
1 large onion, skinned and chopped
1 carrot, scraped and finely chopped (optional)
325 g (12 oz) minced beef
30 ml (2 level tbsp) tomato purée
150 ml ($\frac{1}{4}$ pint) beef stock
salt and freshly ground pepper
225 g (8 oz) spaghetti
30 ml (2 level tbsp) cornflour

Melt the fat in the pressure cooker, add the vegetables and cook for 5 minutes. Add the mince and brown lightly all over. Add the tomato purée, stock and seasoning. Bring to the boil, stirring occasionally. Put the lid on the cooker, bring up to high (15 lb) pressure and cook for 15 minutes. Reduce pressure by the quick method and remove the lid. Meanwhile cook the spaghetti in boiling, salted water for about 12 minutes, until tender. Drain. Blend the cornflour to a smooth paste with a little cold water, add to the sauce and bring to the boil, stirring. Cook until the sauce thickens.
Serving suggestion: grated Parmesan cheese.

☖ Lamb chops with peppers

4 loin lamb chops
salt and freshly ground pepper
25 g (1 oz) butter or margarine
1 large onion, skinned and thinly sliced
3 rashers of streaky bacon, derinded and chopped
1 clove of garlic, skinned and crushed (optional)
rind of 1 lemon, cut into thin strips
30 ml (2 tbsp) lemon juice
5 ml (1 level tsp) sugar
1 red or green pepper, seeded and thinly sliced
10 ml (2 level tsp) paprika
425-g (15-oz) can of tomatoes

Trim the chops and season well. Melt the fat in the pressure cooker and brown the chops on both sides. Remove from the cooker. Add the onion and bacon and cook until the onion is soft, about 5 minutes. Add the remaining ingredients and stir well together. Return the chops to the cooker. Put the lid on the cooker, bring up to high (15 lb) pressure and cook for 15 minutes. Reduce pressure by the quick method. Serve the chops with sauce spooned over.

☖ Summer casserole of lamb

30 ml (2 tbsp) vegetable oil
900 g (2 lb) neck of lamb
300 ml ($\frac{1}{2}$ pint) beef stock
15 ml (1 level tbsp) tomato purée
salt and freshly ground pepper
450 g (1 lb) new carrots, scraped
450 g (1 lb) new potatoes, scraped
225-g (8-oz) packet of frozen peas or fresh shelled peas
15 ml (1 level tbsp) cornflour

Heat the oil in the pressure cooker and lightly fry the meat on all sides; drain off surplus fat. Add the stock, tomato purée and seasoning, bring to the boil, stirring. Put the lid on the cooker, bring up to high (15 lb) pressure and cook for 20 minutes.

Summer casserole of lamb

Reduce pressure by the quick method and remove the lid. Add the carrots and potatoes to the cooker, replace the lid, bring back to high (15 lb) pressure and cook for 5 minutes. Reduce pressure by the quick method and remove the lid. Remove the meat from the cooker, add the peas and continue cooking. Meanwhile remove all bone from the meat, cut into even-sized chunks and return to the cooker. Blend the cornflour to a smooth paste with a little water, add to the cooker, stirring, and continue cooking until the gravy thickens and the peas are tender.

Serving suggestion: mint sauce.

♨ Pork chops in cider

50 g (2 oz) butter or margarine
4 loin pork chops, trimmed
2 crisp green eating apples, cored
300 ml ($\frac{1}{2}$ pint) cider
rind and juice of 1 lemon
salt and pepper
15 ml (1 level tbsp) cornflour or flour

Drink any cider left in the bottle with the meal!

Melt the fat in the pressure cooker and brown the chops on both sides. Remove from the cooker. Cut the apples into 1-cm ($\frac{1}{2}$-in) rings and fry in the same fat until golden brown. Remove these from the cooker and reserve. Return the chops to the cooker, add the cider, lemon rind and seasoning. Bring to the boil, stirring occasionally. Put the lid on the cooker, bring up to high (15 lb) pressure and cook for 20 minutes. Reduce pressure by the quick method and remove the lid. Blend the cornflour to a smooth paste with a little water, add to the cooker with the lemon juice. Bring back to the boil, stirring, and cook until the sauce thickens. Add apple rings and heat through.

♨ Barbecued pork chops

salt and pepper
4 lean spare rib pork chops, trimmed
15 ml (1 tbsp) vegetable oil
15 ml (1 tbsp) clear honey
15 ml (1 tbsp) soy sauce
15 ml (1 level tbsp) tomato ketchup
1 clove of garlic, skinned and crushed (optional)
1·25 ml ($\frac{1}{4}$ level tsp) mustard
15–30 ml (1–2 tbsp) lemon juice
60 ml (4 tbsp) vinegar
150 ml ($\frac{1}{4}$ pint) beef stock
1 small onion, skinned and chopped
15 ml (1 level tbsp) cornflour

Season the chops well. Heat the oil in the pressure cooker and fry the chops until browned on both sides. Drain off excess fat. Mix the remaining ingredients, except the cornflour, together in a bowl and add to the cooker with the onion. Put the lid on the cooker, bring up to high (15 lb) pressure and cook for 20 minutes. Reduce pressure by the quick method and remove the lid. Remove the chops. Blend the cornflour to a smooth paste with a little water, add to the juices in the cooker and cook until the sauce thickens. Add the chops to the sauce and reheat thoroughly.
Serving suggestion: freshly boiled rice.

♨ Boiled bacon

piece of back, gammon or collar bacon, up to 1·8 kg (4 lb) in
  weight
2 onions, skinned and quartered
2 carrots, scraped and quartered
1 bayleaf (optional)
4 peppercorns (optional)
brown breadcrumbs (optional)

Check the weight of the joint. If you are using unsmoked
bacon, place it in the pressure cooker, cover with water, bring
to the boil, drain and proceed as below. If you are using
smoked bacon, soak for at least 2 hours in cold water before
cooking. Place the bacon in the pressure cooker, skin side
down, pour in enough cold water to come halfway up the joint.
Add the onion, carrots, bayleaf, and peppercorns. Bring to the
boil, skimming off any scum that forms. Put the lid on the
cooker, bring up to high (15 lb) pressure and cook, allowing 12
minutes per 450 g (1 lb).

To serve the bacon hot, reduce pressure by the quick
method and remove the lid. Remove the joint from the cooker
and cut away the skin.

Serving suggestion: parsley sauce.

To serve the bacon cold, reduce pressure at room temperature. Remove joint from cooker and cut away the skin. Press
browned breadcrumbs into fat; leave to cool. Serve with salad.

Serving suggestion: mixed salad.

♨ Chicken with lemon cream sauce

4 chicken joints, skinned
salt and pepper
30 ml (2 level tbsp) flour
50 g (2 oz) butter
rind and juice of 1 lemon
1 medium onion, skinned and chopped
90 ml (6 tbsp) dry white wine (optional)
300 ml ($\frac{1}{2}$ pint) chicken stock
15 ml (1 level tbsp) cornflour
60 ml (4 tbsp) single cream or top of the milk

Cut each chicken joint in half and coat in seasoned flour. Melt the butter in the pressure cooker and brown the chicken evenly. Add the lemon juice, onion, wine and stock, bring to the boil, stirring occasionally. Put the lid on the cooker, bring up to high (15 lb) pressure and cook for 15 minutes. Reduce pressure by the quick method and remove the lid. Blend the cornflour to a smooth paste with a little water, add to the cooker with the lemon rind, bring to the boil, stirring continuously, and cook until the sauce thickens. Add the cream and heat through, but do not boil.

Serving suggestion: new potatoes tossed in butter and parsley.

♨ Chicken pot roast with walnuts

1·6 kg (3½ lb) oven-ready chicken
25 g (1 oz) butter or margarine
15 ml (1 tbsp) vegetable oil
2 sticks of celery, washed and sliced (optional)
2 large carrots, scraped and cut into chunks
1 large onion, skinned and chopped
50 g (2 oz) button mushrooms
25 g (1 oz) walnuts
300 ml (½ pint) chicken stock
15 ml (1 level tbsp) cornflour

For the stuffing
knob of butter or margarine
½ small onion, skinned and finely chopped
25 g (1 oz) mushrooms, finely chopped
30 ml (2 level tbsp) chopped walnuts
1 slice of fresh white bread, chopped
5 ml (1 level tsp) dried parsley (optional)
1 egg, beaten
salt and freshly ground pepper

If the family can't do without a Sunday roast – try this tasty pot roast that is cooked in 30 minutes – you'll find it a favourite back home, as well.

To make the stuffing, melt the fat in the pressure cooker, add the onion and mushrooms and sauté until the onion is soft, about 5 minutes. Turn the mixture into a bowl, add the walnuts, bread and parsley; add enough egg to bind the mixture together. Season to taste. Stuff the neck cavity of the chicken.

Melt the fat in the pressure cooker and fry the chicken until brown all over. Remove from the cooker. Add the vegetables and sauté for 5 minutes. Return the chicken to the cooker with the walnuts and stock. Put the lid on the cooker and bring up to high (15 lb) pressure; cook for 20 minutes. Reduce pressure by the quick method and remove the lid. Lift out the chicken and place on a serving dish. Blend the cornflour to a smooth paste with a little water. Add to the juices in the cooker, stirring well. Bring back to the boil, stirring, and cook until the gravy thickens. Serve the chicken with the vegetables and gravy separately.

Serves 4–6

♨ Liver and tomato casserole

325 g (12 oz) lamb's liver
50 g (2 oz) butter or margarine
2 onions, skinned and sliced
2 rashers of bacon, derinded and chopped
425-g (15-oz) can of tomatoes
salt and freshly ground pepper
15 ml (1 level tbsp) cornflour

Cut the liver into 1-cm ($\frac{1}{2}$-in) slices. Melt the fat in the pressure cooker and cook the liver until it is brown on both sides. Remove from the cooker. Add the onion and bacon and cook until the onion is soft, about 5 minutes. Return the liver to the cooker with the tomatoes and seasoning. Put the lid on the cooker, bring up to high (15 lb) pressure and cook for 5 minutes. Reduce pressure by the quick method and remove the lid. Blend the cornflour to a smooth paste with a little water, add to the cooker and bring back to the boil, stirring. Cook until the sauce thickens.

Serving suggestion: freshly cooked spaghetti or rice.

♨ Goulash soup

325 g (12 oz) stewing steak or leg of beef
5 ml (1 level tsp) salt
freshly ground black pepper
25 g (1 oz) butter or margarine
1 large onion, skinned and chopped
226-g (8-oz) can of tomatoes
63-g ($2\frac{1}{4}$-oz) can of tomato purée
600 ml (1 pint) beef stock
15 ml (1 level tbsp) paprika pepper
450 g (1 lb) potatoes, peeled
142-ml (5-fl oz) carton of soured or single cream (optional)

Trim meat and cut into 1·25-cm ($\frac{1}{2}$-in) cubes. Season well. Melt the fat in the pressure cooker, add the onion and cook until soft, about 5 minutes. Add meat, tomatoes, tomato purée, beef stock and paprika to the cooker. Stir to blend the ingredients together. Put the lid on the cooker, bring up to high (15 lb) pressure and cook for 15 minutes. Reduce pressure by the quick method. Remove the lid. Cut the potatoes into bite-size pieces, add to the soup. Put the lid on the cooker, bring back to high (15 lb) pressure and cook for 4–5 minutes. Reduce pressure by the quick method. Serve soup with a swirl of soured cream in each portion.

♨ Veal goulash

25 g (1 oz) butter or margarine
450 g (1 lb) pie veal, cut into cubes
1 large onion, skinned and sliced
1 large green pepper, seeded and sliced
30 ml (2 level tbsp) paprika
226-g (8-oz) can of tomatoes
300 ml ($\frac{1}{2}$ pint) chicken stock
pinch of nutmeg (optional)
2·5 ml ($\frac{1}{2}$ level tsp) dried sage (optional)
salt and freshly ground pepper
15 ml (1 level tbsp) cornflour
142-ml (5-fl oz) carton of soured or single cream (optional)

Melt the fat in the pressure cooker and fry the meat until golden. Remove from the cooker. Add the onion and pepper and cook until the onion is soft, about 5 minutes. Stir in the paprika and cook for 1 minute, stirring. Add the tomatoes, stock, nutmeg, sage and seasoning. Return the meat to the pressure cooker and bring to the boil, stirring. Put the lid on the cooker, bring up to high (15 lb) pressure and cook for 20 minutes. Reduce pressure by the quick method and remove the lid. Blend the cornflour to a smooth paste with a little water, add to the cooker, bring back to the boil, stirring, and cook until the sauce thickens. Serve with soured cream.

Serving suggestion: boiled rice or noodles.

Curried cod chowder

50 g (2 oz) butter or margarine
1 large onion, skinned and chopped
2 sticks of celery, trimmed and chopped
5 ml (1 level tbsp) curry powder
45 ml (3 level tbsp) flour
300 ml ($\frac{1}{2}$ pint) milk
900 ml ($1\frac{1}{2}$ pints) chicken stock
325 g (12 oz) cod fillet or other white fish, skinned
2 large potatoes, peeled and diced
salt and pepper
15 ml (1 tbsp) chopped parsley and chives (optional)

Melt the fat in the pressure cooker, add the onion and celery and cook until the onion is soft, about 5 minutes. Stir in the curry powder and the flour and cook for 1 minute, stirring all the time. Remove the cooker from the heat, gradually stir in the milk and stock. Cut the fish into 2·5-cm (1-in) cubes and add with the potatotes and seasoning. Stir to blend the ingredients. Put the lid on the cooker, bring up to high (15 lb) pressure and cook for 3–4 minutes. Reduce pressure by the quick method. Remove the lid, stir in the parsley and chives and serve immediately.

Serving suggestion: French bread.

Super sweets

QUICK ICE CREAM DISHES

Mocha nut sundae

Divide a coffee ice cream block between serving dishes. Pour 15 ml (1 tbsp) bottled chocolate sauce over each portion and top with chopped walnuts or almonds.

Cherry crunch sundae

Crush 4–6 digestive biscuits and divide them between serving dishes. Divide a vanilla ice cream block and place on top. Spoon a can of cherry pie filling over the ice cream.

Quick pears Hélène

Divide a vanilla ice cream block between serving dishes. Decorate with canned pear halves and pour bottled chocolate sauce over the top.

Chocolate mint sauce for ice cream

Melt 10–12 mint chocolates in a basin over hot water. Stir in a

Mocha nut sundae

142-ml (5-fl oz) carton of soured or double cream and continue heating until smooth. Stir in 15 ml (1 tbsp) water and pour over vanilla ice cream.

Coffee cream sauce for ice cream

Dissolve 10 ml (2 level tsp) coffee powder in 10 ml (2 tsp) hot water, cool and stir into a 142-ml (5-fl oz) carton of double cream. Pour over vanilla or chocolate ice cream.

◊ Ice cream fiesta

4 trifle sponges
60 ml (4 tbsp) sherry
10 ml (2 level tsp) arrowroot or cornflour
60 ml (4 tbsp) rosehip syrup or red jam
120 ml (8 tbsp) water
225 g (8 oz) fresh strawberries, washed, hulled and sliced
4 individual blocks of ice cream
chopped nuts (optional)

Split the sponges in half and arrange the sponge bases on four serving plates. Sprinkle each sponge with sherry. In a small pan combine the arrowroot, syrup or jam and water together. Bring to the boil, stirring continuously. Cool; fold in the strawberries when lukewarm. Place the ice cream on top of the sponge bases and sandwich with the sponge tops. Pour sauce over the sponge tops and sprinkle with chopped nuts.

Apricot and almond cream

425-g (15-oz) can of apricots
142-ml (5-fl oz) carton of soured or double cream
30 ml (2 level tbsp) soft brown sugar
50 g (2 oz) flaked almonds, toasted

Divide the apricots between four serving dishes and add 15 ml

(1 tbsp) of the juice to each. Stir the cream and brown sugar together, spoon over the apricots. Scatter almonds over the cream. Chill if possible before serving.

☖ Apple crunch surprise

2·5 ml ($\frac{1}{2}$ level tsp) cinnamon
396-g (14-oz) can of apple pie filling
25 g (1 oz) butter
3 slices of bread, crusts removed and cut into small cubes
113-g (4-oz) can of cream or 142-ml (5-fl oz) carton of double cream
5 ml (1 level tsp) sugar
grated rind and juice of $\frac{1}{2}$ lemon

If you use the can of cream this is a pudding you can make straight from the storecupboard.

Stir the cinnamon into the apple and divide between four dishes. Melt the butter in a pan, add the bread cubes and cook until golden. Spoon on to the apple and leave to cool. Shake the can of cream and turn into a bowl or whip the double cream; add the sugar, lemon rind and juice and stir well. Spoon the cream over the bread cubes and serve.

Strawberries with macaroons

75-g (3-oz) packet of macaroons
30 ml (2 tbsp) sherry (optional)
30 ml (2 tbsp) fresh orange juice
225 g (8 oz) fresh strawberries, washed
sugar
142-ml (5-fl oz) carton of double cream

Reserve four macaroons and divide the remainder between four serving dishes. Sprinkle with the sherry and orange juice and leave until the macaroons have absorbed most of the liquid. Reserve four strawberries. Hull the remainder and slice, divide between four dishes and dust with sugar. Whip the cream until it holds its shape, pile on top of the strawberries and decorate with the reserved macaroons and strawberries.

Strawberries with pineapple cream

226-g (8-oz) can of pineapple pieces
225 g (8 oz) fresh strawberries, washed and hulled
caster sugar
15 ml (1 tbsp) sherry or wine (optional)
142-ml (5-fl oz) carton of soured or double cream
10 ml (2 level tsp) soft brown sugar

Cook the pineapple in a small, uncovered pan until the juice
has evaporated and the pineapple is transparent. Cool. Divide
the strawberries between four serving dishes, sprinkle with
the sugar and sherry or wine. Whip the cream until thick and
carefully fold in the pineapple and sugar. Pile on top of the
strawberries and leave to cool before serving.

Pineapple chocolate crunch

50 g (2 oz) butter
100 g (4 oz) plain chocolate
50 g (2 oz) golden syrup or honey
50 g (2 oz) cornflakes
25 g (1 oz) walnuts, chopped
226-g (8-oz) can of pineapple pieces, drained
142-ml (5-fl oz) carton of double cream (optional)

Place the butter, chocolate and syrup in a saucepan and heat
gently until smooth, stirring occasionally. Stir in the cornflakes, walnuts and pineapple pieces. Turn the mixture into an
18-cm (7-in) sandwich tin or similar container, press down well
and leave until cold and set. Whip the cream, if used. Turn out
the pineapple crunch, spread with cream and cut into wedges.

Lemon and grape creams

142-ml (5-fl oz) carton of double cream
two 141-g (5-oz) cartons of lemon yoghurt
rind and juice of 1 lemon
100 g (4 oz) grapes

Whip the cream until it holds its shape. Gently fold in the yoghurt, lemon rind and juice. Halve the grapes, discard the pips and reserve a few for garnishing. Stir the grapes into the yoghurt mixture. Divide between four serving dishes and top with the reserved grapes.

⚠ Summer holiday pudding

450 g (1 lb) soft fruit – raspberries, blackcurrants,
    blackberries, strawberries, etc
sugar
thin slices of white bread
cream to serve (optional)

Stew the fruit very gently with sugar to taste, until tender. Arrange the fruit and bread in layers in a pudding basin or suitable container, finishing with a layer of bread. Pour over any remaining juice from the fruit. Cover the pudding with a plate, place a can or some other heavy weight on top. Leave for $1\frac{1}{2}$–$2\frac{1}{2}$ hours or overnight. Turn out, if preferred, and serve with fresh cream.
Serves 4–6

⚠ Peach en croûte

8 thin slices of brown bread
50 g (2 oz) butter
30 ml (2 level tbsp) caster sugar
5 ml (1 level tsp) cinnamon (optional)
4 fresh peaches, halved and stoned
142-ml (5-fl oz) carton of single cream

Remove the crusts from the bread. Melt the butter in a frying pan and fry the bread until golden on both sides. Stir together the sugar and cinnamon, if used, and toss each slice of fried bread in sugar until well coated. Add the peach halves to the pan and fry for 1 minute. Serve the cinnamon bread topped with peach halves and cream.

Peach condé

425-g (15-oz) can of creamed rice
425-g (15-oz) can of peach halves, drained
120 ml (8 tbsp) redcurrant jelly or red jam
15 ml (1 tbsp) water
15 ml (1 tbsp) lemon juice

Spoon the rice into four serving dishes and top with peach halves. Place the redcurrant jelly, water and lemon juice in a saucepan, heat gently until dissolved. Cool slightly. Spoon over the peaches and leave until cold.

Raspberry sponge meringue

1 jam Swiss roll
225 g (8 oz) raspberries, stewed with a little sugar or a 425-g
    (15-oz) can of raspberries
2 egg whites
30 ml (2 level tbsp) sugar

Slice the Swiss roll into eight even slices and arrange it in the base of an ovenproof dish. Spoon the raspberries and juice over the base and leave the slices to soak up the juice. Whisk the egg whites until stiff, then whisk in the sugar. Pile the meringue mixture on top of the raspberry base and brown under a hot grill.

Apple snow trifle

4 trifle sponges
425-g (15-oz) can of custard
113-g (4-oz) can of apple purée *
75 g (3 oz) caster sugar
lemon juice
1 egg, separated
glacé cherries to decorate (optional)

* For the apple purée use either a can of apple sauce or strained apple baby food.

Place the trifle sponges in the base of individual dishes. Pour the custard over them and allow to soak for a few minutes. Meanwhile stir the apple, sugar, lemon juice and egg yolk together. Whisk the egg white until stiff and fold into the apple mixture. Pile on top of the custard and decorate with cherries.

♨ Apricot cheesecake

175 g (6 oz) digestive biscuits, crushed
15 ml (1 level tbsp) granulated sugar
75 g (3 oz) melted butter
170-g (6-oz) can of evaporated milk, preferably cold
225 g (8 oz) full fat soft cream cheese
50 g (2 oz) caster sugar
finely grated rind and juice of 1 lemon
425-g (15-oz) can of apricots, drained

Crush the biscuits in a bag. Combine the crushed biscuits, granulated sugar and butter together. Turn into an 18-cm (7-in) loose bottomed cake tin or similar container. Whisk the evaporated milk until it is pale and thick. Combine the cream cheese, caster sugar, lemon rind and juice and beat well. Fold the evaporated milk into the cream cheese mixture. Pour on to the biscuit base and leave in a cool place to set. Top with apricot halves.
Serves 4–6

♨ Quick chocolate soufflé

100 g (4 oz) plain chocolate
knob of butter
4 eggs, separated
toasted flaked almonds to decorate (optional)
single cream (optional)

Place the chocolate and butter in a basin over a pan of hot water. Heat gently until the chocolate has melted. Remove the basin from the heat, cool slightly and stir in the egg yolks. Whisk the egg whites until stiff and gently fold into the chocolate mixture. Divide the mixture between four serving dishes and leave to set. Decorate with nuts or serve with a little single cream.

♨ Glazed bananas

75 g (3 oz) butter
45 ml (3 level tbsp) brown sugar
5 ml (1 tsp) lemon juice
1·25 ml ($\frac{1}{4}$ level tsp) cinnamon (optional)
4 bananas

Place the butter, sugar, lemon juice and cinnamon in a frying pan. Heat until the butter melts, stirring occasionally. Peel the bananas and cut in half, lengthways. Add the bananas to the pan and cook for 5 minutes on each side, until soft and well glazed.
Serving suggestion: vanilla ice cream or whipped double cream.

♨ Pineapple rice

425-g (15-oz) can of creamed rice
226-g (8-oz) can of pineapple slices
25 g (1 oz) sugar
glacé cherries to decorate (optional)

Divide the rice between four dishes. Drain the juice from the pineapple and boil it rapidly in a small pan with the sugar until it reaches a syrupy consistency, about 10 minutes. Arrange the pineapple slices on top of the rice and place the cherries in the centre. Spoon the pineapple glaze over the dessert and leave to cool.

Cooking on barbecues and camp fires

There is nothing more appetising than the smell of fresh food being cooked over a barbecue or open fire on a hot summer evening. Kebabs are particularly easy to prepare and perfect for trying new combinations of flavours. Simply thread tender chunks of meat or fish on to a pointed skewer or green stick, together with vegetables or fruit – quartered onions, halved tomatoes, pieces of red or green pepper, chunky slices of courgette, bacon rolls stuffed with prunes, slices of lemon or orange, peach or apricot halves, pineapple cubes, the variety is enormous. For a really tasty kebab the meat should first be marinaded, then basted well during the cooking with oil, butter or one of the bastes on pages 114–115. Serve kebabs with freshly cooked rice and plenty of salad or, for easy outdoor eating, simply slide the cooked food from the skewer onto a hollowed out soft bap or a piece of French bread.

If you have made a good barbecue or fire, you will probably find that even after the food for your main course has been cooked, eaten and enjoyed the embers are still throwing out plenty of heat. Don't waste time or effort – make the family a delicious hot barbecued dessert. Thread a combination of fresh or canned fruit on to skewers and cook it over the embers for a few minutes. You will find recipes for barbecued desserts on the following pages.

To prepare the barbecue or fire (see pages 35–37)
Prepare the barbecue or fire well in advance, allowing about an hour. When lighting charcoal use wood and paper or firelighters – don't encourage the fire by adding petrol or methylated spirit – not only is it a fire risk but the smell will taint the food.

Before you cook the kebabs or other foods, make sure the barbecue or fire is ready. The flames should have died down and the charcoal should have stopped smoking – the cooking is actually done on a bed of glowing embers. If you are cooking

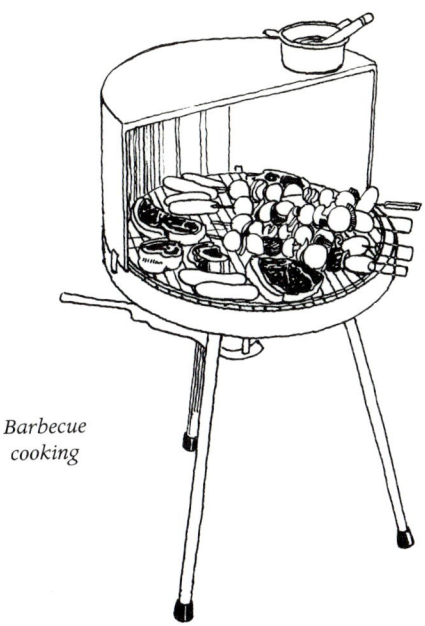

Barbecue
cooking

on charcoal in daylight, it is difficult to tell if you have achieved glowing embers, they will in fact be whitish-grey and look rather dead.

Marinades

All meats and fish are improved by marinading before they are cooked on the barbecue or fire. The marinade not only brings out the flavour in the meat or fish but actually helps to tenderise it. Different meats and fish are marinaded for varying times. Allow about 3–4 hours for lamb, about 2 hours for pork; beef can be successfully marinaded for as little as 30 minutes if it is cubed; allow about 1 hour for fish. Obviously circumstances will determine how much time you have to marinade food while on holiday but even a short marinade is better than none. The choice of marinades is extremely wide and the combinations of flavour can be altered to suit your family's taste, but to start with you might like to try one of the following. Make enough marinade almost to cover the amount of meat or fish used.

A marinade or baste for beef

150 ml ($\frac{1}{4}$ pint) vegetable oil
1 clove of garlic, skinned and crushed
5 ml (1 tsp) Worcestershire sauce
5 ml (1 level tsp) curry powder
5 ml (1 level tsp) salt
1·25 ml ($\frac{1}{4}$ level tsp) ground pepper
30 ml (2 tbsp) lemon juice
15 ml (1 tbsp) cider vinegar

Combine all the ingredients together in a large bowl. Trim the excess fat from the meat, add to the bowl and spoon marinade over the meat to coat each piece thoroughly. Cover and leave in a cool place for $\frac{1}{2}$–1 hour. This will marinade four 175–225 g (6–8 oz) steaks. When the meat has been marinaded, use the surplus juices as a baste during cooking (see page 115).

A spicy marinade for pork or lamb

60 ml (4 tbsp) soy sauce
60 ml (4 tbsp) clear honey
120 ml (8 tbsp) water
ground or freshly grated ginger
60 ml (4 tbsp) red wine

Combine all the ingredients together in a large bowl. Trim the excess fat from the meat and cut it into 2·5-cm (1-in) cubes, add to the bowl and spoon the marinade over the meat, coating each cube thoroughly. Cover and leave in a cool place for 2–3 hours. This will marinade 900 g (2 lb) pork or lamb.

Other delicious marinades

For lamb
equal amounts of oil and lemon juice.
dry white wine, herbs and crushed garlic.
yoghurt, herbs and garlic.

For veal
equal amounts of oil and lemon juice; thyme, crumpled bayleaves, rosemary, salt.

For pork
soy sauce, honey, sherry and a hint of garlic.
a spicy one – soy sauce, lemon juice, onion, coriander, cumin, brown sugar and ground ginger.

For chicken
oil, lemon juice, parsley, thyme, chopped celery leaves.

For beef
equal amounts of oil and red wine, plus tomato juice, Worcestershire sauce, soy sauce.

For white fish
oil, dry white wine, garlic, onion, parsley, oregano, salt and pepper.

Bastes

The aim of cooking over an open fire is to retain the natural flavour and succulent juices of the food. Basting enhances the natural flavour and protects the food from overcooking on the outside. Don't blend too many different flavours together – the simplest combinations are usually the best. Make the baste quite syrupy, so that it sticks to the food and does not immediately run off. Some foods can be basted from the beginning of the cooking time, but bastes containing tomato purée or sauce should be used towards the end of the cooking time, as tomato tends to brown very quickly. Soy sauce diluted with an equal amount of water gives an interesting flavour. A little honey added to the mixture will help coat the food and give a beautiful rich golden colour. Fish and chicken flavours are specially enhanced by a baste of lemon or lime juice with butter and freshly chopped herbs. You can also use the surplus juices from the marinade as a baste.

Shish kebabs

450 g (1 lb) boned leg or shoulder of lamb
4 small courgettes, trimmed and thickly sliced
8 small tomatoes
2 medium onions, skinned and quartered
bayleaves

For the marinade
150 ml ($\frac{1}{4}$ pint) vegetable oil
1 clove of garlic, skinned and crushed
1 small onion, skinned and finely chopped
salt and freshly ground pepper
30 ml (2 tbsp) lemon juice

Blend the marinade ingredients together. Cut the meat into 2·5-cm (1-in) cubes, add to the marinade and stir to coat well. Cover and leave in a cool place to marinade, preferably overnight. Drain the meat, reserving the marinade. Thread the meat, courgettes, tomatoes, onion and bayleaves on to eight skewers. Brush well with the remaining marinade and cook on a prepared barbecue or fire for 20–30 minutes, turning and basting frequently.

Gammon and pineapple kebabs

450 g (1 lb) gammon slices 1 cm ($\frac{1}{2}$ in) thick
425-g (15-oz) can of pineapple cubes
1 green pepper, seeded
100 g (4 oz) button mushrooms
8 bayleaves
30 ml (2 tbsp) clear honey
10 ml (2 tsp) soy sauce

Cut the gammon into 1-cm ($\frac{1}{2}$-in) cubes. Drain the pineapple and reserve juice. Cut the pepper into eight pieces. Thread the gammon and pineapple cubes, pepper, mushrooms and bayleaves on to four skewers. Blend the pineapple juice with the honey and soy sauce and brush the kebabs with the sauce. Cook over a prepared barbecue or open fire for 15–20 minutes, turning and basting occasionally.
Serving suggestion: freshly boiled rice.

Minced meat shashliks

450 g (1 lb) minced beef
5 ml (1 level tsp) salt
1·25 ml ($\frac{1}{4}$ level tsp) pepper
15 ml (1 level tbsp) onion, grated or finely chopped
15 ml (1 tbsp) Worcestershire sauce
12 baby onions, peeled, or 3 medium onions, skinned and
    quartered
bayleaves
vegetable oil
2 tomatoes, halved

Combine the mince, salt, pepper, grated onion and Worcester-shire sauce well together. Shape the mixture into small balls about the size of a walnut. Thread the meatballs, baby onions and bayleaves on to four skewers, brush with oil and cook on prepared barbecue or fire for 10–15 minutes, turning occasionally. Add the tomato halves to the skewers and cook for a further 5 minutes.

Barbecued chicken

1·1–1·4-kg (2$\frac{1}{2}$–3 lb) oven-ready chicken
50–75 g (2–3 oz) butter
salt and freshly ground pepper

If you are using a frozen chicken make sure it is thoroughly thawed before starting. Cut the chicken in half along the breast bone, wash and dry each half thoroughly. Soften the butter if necessary, season well and spread the skin side of the chicken with half the butter. Cook, skin side down, over a prepared barbecue or fire for 20–30 minutes, until the skin is golden brown. Turn the chicken halves over, season and smear the second side with the remaining butter. Continue cooking for a further 20–30 minutes. Test the chicken by piercing the leg joint with a skewer or sharp knife: if the chicken is cooked the liquid from the bird will be clear – if it is still tinted with blood continue cooking.
Serving suggestion: a selection of salads or Devilled sweetcorn (see page 121).

Cheese sausage rolls

4 slices of processed Cheddar Cheese
20 ml (4 level tsp) tomato ketchup
8 rashers of smoked streaky bacon, derinded
8 thick pork sausages
8 long soft rolls or baps

Cut the cheese slices in half diagonally and spread with tomato ketchup. Stretch the bacon rashers with the back of a knife. Wrap a cheese slice around each sausage, tomato side next to the sausage. Overwrap each with a bacon rasher and thread on to a skewer, making sure the ends of the bacon are well secured. Cook over prepared barbecue or fire for 20–30 minutes turning frequently until the sausages are cooked and the bacon is crisp. While the sausages are cooking, split the rolls in half and toast on the cut side. Serve the sausages sandwiched between the rolls.
Makes 8

Mackerel with mustard butter cooked in foil

75 g (3 oz) butter, softened
30 ml (2 level tbsp) French mustard
15 ml (1 level tbsp) dried parsley (optional)
salt and freshly ground black pepper
2 mackerel or herrings, cleaned and with heads removed
lemon wedges

Combine 50 g (2 oz) butter, mustard, parsley and seasoning. Cut two pieces of foil large enough to wrap around each fish. Spread a little mustard butter on the base of the foil. Fill the cavity of each fish with mustard butter. Make three diagonal slits in each side of the fish and place in the foil. Spread remaining butter on top of the fish and make a parcel, sealing it tightly. Place the parcels in the embers of the fire and cook for 15–20 minutes, turning once. Serve the fish and juices with lemon wedges.
Serves 2

Mackerel with mustard butter cooked in foil

Beefburger skewers

8 beefburgers, fresh or frozen
French mustard
8 tomatoes
salt and pepper
4 courgettes, trimmed
2 large onions, skinned
vegetable oil

Spread each beefburger with mustard and cut into four. Cut the tomatoes in half and season; cut each courgette into eight thick slices and season; cut the onions into quarters and season. Thread the ingredients alternately on to eight skewers, brush the vegetables with oil and cook over a prepared barbecue or fire for 15–20 minutes, turning occasionally and brushing with more oil if required.
Serving suggestion: crusty French bread and green salad.
Makes 8

Honey glazed chicken with bananas

4 chicken joints
vegetable oil
60 ml (4 tbsp) clear honey
15 ml (1 level tbsp) French mustard
10 ml (2 tbsp) Worcestershire sauce
freshly ground black pepper
2 firm bananas

Cut each chicken joint into two or three pieces. Brush with oil and cook over a prepared barbecue or fire for 10 minutes. Mix the honey, mustard, Worcestershire sauce and pepper together and glaze the chicken pieces with the mixture. Continue cooking, turning and glazing the chicken pieces, until well browned and crisp. Peel and slice the bananas into four or five thick slices. Thread on to a skewer and cook over the barbecue or fire for about 5 minutes.

Turkish fish kebabs

325 g (12 oz) cod fillet, skinned
1 red or green pepper, halved and seeded
2 rashers of back bacon, derinded
16 button mushrooms
8 bayleaves
two 141-g (5-oz) cartons of natural yoghurt
5 ml (1 level tsp) chilli seasoning
2·5 ml ($\frac{1}{2}$ level tsp) ground ginger (optional)

Cut the cod into sixteen pieces. Cut the pepper into twelve pieces. Stretch the bacon rashers with the back of a knife and cut each into six pieces. Fold each piece in half. Thread the cod, mushrooms, red or green pepper, bacon bits and bayleaves on to four skewers. Combine the yoghurt, chilli and ginger together in a bowl. Arrange the kebabs in a flat dish, pour the yoghurt mixture over the kebabs and leave to marinade while preparing the barbecue or fire. Cook the kebabs, turning and basting with yoghurt mixture regularly for about 15–20 minutes.
Serving suggestion: salad and crusty bread rolls.

Veal kebabs

450 g (1 lb) shoulder veal
2 medium onions, skinned and quartered
2 firm tomatoes, halved
1 green pepper, seeded and cut into eight pieces
paprika or freshly ground black pepper
garlic salt (optional)
30 ml (2 tbsp) vegetable oil

For the marinade
141-g (5-oz) carton of natural yoghurt
1 medium onion, skinned and finely chopped
salt and freshly ground pepper

Blend the ingredients for the marinade together. Cut the veal into 2·5-cm (1-in) pieces, add to the marinade, stir well and coat evenly. Cover and leave to marinade in a cool place for about 2 hours.

Drain the meat, reserving the marinade, and thread on to four skewers with the onion, tomato and pepper, season with pepper and garlic salt. Brush with oil and cook over a prepared barbecue or fire for about 20–30 minutes, turning and brushing with oil frequently. Serve kebabs with the marinade poured over them.

Devilled sweetcorn

2 medium-size fresh or frozen* corn cobs
100 g (4 oz) butter or margarine
60 ml (4 level tbsp) sweet pickle
5 ml (1 tsp) lemon juice
5 ml (1 level tsp) chopped parsley
salt and freshly ground pepper

Remove the silk and outer leaves from the corn cobs, trim if necessary. Blanch in boiling water for about 6 minutes, drain. Soften the fat if necessary, combine with the pickle, lemon juice, parsley and seasoning. Spread each cob all over with half of the mixture. Wrap each cob in foil, seal well and cook in the

* If frozen cobs are used they need not be blanched

embers of a prepared barbecue or fire for 20–30 minutes until the corn is tender.
Makes 2

Liver and bacon brochettes

225 g (8 oz) lamb's liver
salt and freshly ground pepper
15 ml (1 level tbsp) flour
6 rashers of lean bacon
1 large orange
100 g (4 oz) mushrooms
vegetable oil

Cut the liver into 2·5-cm (1-in) cubes and coat in seasoned flour. Remove the rind and any bone from the bacon rashers, cut each in half, stretch with the back of a knife and roll up. Remove the skin and all the pith from the orange, cut into eight pieces. Arrange the liver cubes, bacon, orange and mushrooms on eight skewers, brush with oil and cook over a prepared barbecue or fire for 15–20 minutes, turning and brushing with oil occasionally.

Seafood skewers

225 g (8 oz) cod fillet, skinned
100 g (4 oz) peeled prawns
100 g (4 oz) streaky bacon, derinded
4 courgettes, washed and trimmed
1 lemon, sliced

For the marinade
60 ml (4 tbsp) vegetable oil
150 ml ($\frac{1}{4}$ pint) dry white wine
30 ml (2 tbsp) lemon juice
salt and freshly ground pepper

Cut the cod into 2·5-cm (1-in) cubes. Wash the prawns and drain well. Cut any bone from bacon and stretch each rasher with the back of a knife. Cut each rasher into four pieces. Wrap each prawn in a piece of bacon. Thickly slice courgettes. Thread the cod, the bacon-wrapped prawns, courgettes and lemon slices on four skewers. Arrange the skewers in a shallow dish.

Stir the ingredients for the marinade together and pour over the seafood skewers. Cover and leave to marinade while preparing the barbecue or fire. Cook over the prepared barbecue or fire for 10–15 minutes, turning and basting occasionally.

Ginger glazed lamb skewers

450 g (1 lb) boned leg or shoulder of lamb

For the marinade
45 ml (3 level tbsp) stem ginger, chopped
15 ml (1 tbsp) soy sauce
15 ml (1 level tbsp) tomato purée
2 spring onions, chopped
90 ml (6 tbsp) white stock
salt and freshly ground pepper

Cut the meat into bite-size pieces and place in a shallow dish. Combine the marinade ingredients together in a small pan and heat gently for 5 minutes. Pour over the meat, cover and leave to marinade, preferably overnight.

Drain the meat, thread on to four skewers and cook over a prepared barbecue or fire for 20–30 minutes, brushing with the marinade and turning frequently. Heat any remaining marinade separately and serve with the lamb skewers.

Trout with almonds

4 medium-size trout
50 g (2 oz) butter, softened
50 g (2 oz) flaked almonds
rind and juice of 1 lemon

Clean and wash the fish and spread both sides with butter. Make four cups with double foil, each large enough to hold one fish. Place a fish in each cup and cook over a prepared barbecue

or fire for 15–20 minutes, turning once. Add the almonds to the melted butter in the cups and cook until golden. Spoon lemon rind and juice over the trout and heat through. Serve the trout with the almonds and juice.

Spanish style sardines

16 sardines or sprats
16 bayleaves

For the marinade
1 medium onion, chopped
60 ml (4 tbsp) oil
150 ml ($\frac{1}{4}$ pint) dry white wine
1 lemon, sliced

Remove the heads from the fish, slit open and remove the backbone. Place a bayleaf in each fish and fold the two halves together. Thread the fish on to four skewers and arrange in a shallow dish. Stir the ingredients for the marinade together and pour over the fish. Cover and leave to marinade while preparing the barbecue or fire. Cook over the prepared barbecue or fire for 15–20 minutes, turning and basting occasionally.

BARBECUED FRUIT

Pineapple and cherry kebabs

439-g (15$\frac{1}{2}$-oz) can of pineapple cubes
100 g (4 oz) fresh or glacé cherries
142-ml (5-fl oz) carton of double or soured cream

Drain the pineapple, reserving the juice. Wash the fresh cherries, if used, and stone if you prefer. Thread the pineapple cubes and cherries on to four skewers. Brush well with pineapple juice and cook over a prepared barbecue or fire for 5–10 minutes, turning and basting occasionally. Remove the fruit from the skewers and serve with cream.

Barbecued bananas

4 firm bananas
30 ml (2 tbsp) honey
15 ml (1 tbsp) lemon juice
30 ml (2 level tbsp) soft brown sugar
melted butter

Peel the bananas and cut them in half lengthways. Stir the honey, lemon juice and sugar together. Spread one half of each banana with the mixture and sandwich together with the other half. Thread each banana on to a skewer. Brush the banana with melted butter and cook over a prepared barbecue or open fire for 5–10 minutes, until golden.

Stuffed apples in foil

4 medium-size cooking apples
grated rind and juice of 1 lemon
60 ml (4 level tbsp) mincemeat or brown sugar and sultanas
425-g (15-oz) can of custard

Cut four pieces of foil, each large enough to wrap around an apple. Core the apples and stand each in the centre of a piece of foil. Stir the lemon rind and juice into the mincemeat and stuff the apples. Wrap up each apple in foil, seal and cook in the embers of a prepared barbecue or fire for 15–20 minutes, until tender. Open a can of custard cover with foil and stand the can among embers to heat.

Tipsy grapefruit

2 large grapefruit
50 g (2 oz) glacé cherries
50 g (2 oz) nuts, chopped
30 ml (2 level tbsp) soft brown sugar
60 ml (4 tbsp) sherry or sweet red or white wine

Cut each grapefruit in half and place cut side down on a grid over a prepared barbecue or fire. Cook for 10–15 minutes until golden. Remove the grapefruit from the fire and quickly loosen the segments; return to the fire, cut side up. Stir the cherries, nuts and sugar together and spoon on to the grapefruit halves. Sprinkle each half with sherry or wine and heat through.

Peach creams with wholemeal fingers

50 g (2 oz) butter, softened
30 ml (2 level tbsp) soft brown sugar
8 slices of wholemeal bread
4 large fresh peaches
142-ml (5-fl oz) carton of soured or double cream

Stir the butter and sugar together and spread on four slices of bread, make into sandwiches with the remaining slices of bread. Remove the crusts. Cut the peaches in half, remove the stones and thread two halves on to each skewer. Toast sandwiches on both sides until golden brown; cut into fingers. Cook the peaches on the prepared barbecue or fire for 5–10 minutes. Remove the peaches from the skewers and serve topped with cream and wholemeal fingers.

FONDUES

Fondues are quick and simple to cook over a barbecue or open fire as everyone does his own cooking and serves himself. Prepare a large tray or bowl of different foods to dip into the fondue – cubes of pineapples, cucumber, ham, wholemeal or French bread, mushrooms, celery, cauliflower florets, sticks of carrot, pickled onions, radishes, slices of crisp eating apple.

As the fondue cools it gets thicker. If necessary, place it back on the barbecue or fire and reheat.

Cider fondue

300 ml ($\frac{1}{2}$ pint) dry cider
450 g (1 lb) Gruyère cheese, grated or cut into small cubes
30 ml (2 level tbsp) flour
salt and pepper
pinch of nutmeg (optional)

Gently heat the cider in a large thick-based pan. Mix the cheese and flour together and add to the pan gradually, stirring until all the cheese has melted. Stir in the seasoning and nutmeg and cook until the fondue thickens. Serve immediately with any combination of the foods mentioned on page 126.

Farmhouse fondue

1 clove of garlic
450 g (1 lb) farmhouse Cheddar cheese, grated or cut into
　small cubes
150 ml ($\frac{1}{4}$ pint) milk
salt and pepper
pinch of dry mustard
pinch of nutmeg (optional)
30 ml (2 tbsp) dry white wine (optional)

Rub the inside of a large, thick-based pan with garlic. Add the cheese and melt carefully, stirring continuously. Stir in the remaining ingredients and cook until thick and creamy. Serve immediately with any combination of the foods mentioned on page 126.

Blue cheese fondue

400 ml ($\frac{3}{4}$ pint) beer
5 ml (1 level tsp) grated or finely chopped onion
50 g (2 oz) blue cheese, crumbled
325 g (12 oz) Cheddar cheese, grated or cut into small cubes
15 ml (1 level tbsp) flour

Heat the beer and onion in a large thick-based pan. Add the blue cheese and stir until it melts. Mix the Cheddar cheese and flour together and gradually add to the mixture, stirring until each addition has melted and the fondue thickens. Serve immediately with any combination of the foods suggested on page 126.

Food from the fields and markets

If you are holidaying in the country or near the sea, take the opportunity to sample nature's food – it is there for the picking. Once you become aware of the plants and trees around you, you will be amazed at the number of fruits and berries that are not only edible but often infinitely superior in flavour and texture to their cultivated relations. When you have tasted fresh field mushrooms, blackberry salad or elderberry sauce your eyes will automatically watch out for food from the countryside. You may even feel that cooking a few bilberries for a quick dessert is really a waste when pounds of berries remain on the bushes. If so, return to the treasured spot on the last day of your holiday and set the family picking as many as possible. Store your hoard in a cool, dry place overnight – underneath the caravan is always a cool spot – and make it into preserves when you get home. What a lovely way to remember your holiday: instead of showing off holiday snaps you can pass the bilberry jelly!

FRUIT

Recipes for jams and jellies, etc, are to be made at home
When gathering berries from the hedgerow, try and avoid those that are near the roadside and have been polluted by the exhaust fumes of passing lorries and cars and those that are growing low on the bushes that may have been visited by dogs or local wildlife. Pick only fruit in prime condition, sound and just ripe. If you are picking fruit for jam or jelly pick under-ripe rather than over-ripe, as the pectin content is higher in under-ripe fruit and this means a better setting jam. If you are storing quantities of fruit to take home and make into jam,

don't wash or sort them until you arrive home – moisture encourages decomposition.

Bilberry, Whortleberry or Blaeberry (the name varies depending on where you are). This deciduous, low-growing shrub with green angular twigs and oval leaves is found all over Britain except East Anglia and is most abundant in the north. The plant is easy to identify. It has strawberry red bell flowers in early spring and summer and sweet blue black berries in July and August. The berries have a powdery bloom just like grapes and ripen as the leaves turn yellow and purple.

Eat really ripe berries raw with sugar and plenty of cream or yoghurt or if you prefer stew gently with a little sugar until just tender and try them as a filling for pancakes. If you can take the berries home, rub them through a sieve or liquidise them, then sweeten them with caster sugar to make a purée, add equal quantities of stiffly whipped cream to make a bilberry fool. Alternatively, freeze the mixture to make bilberry ice cream. A traditional Lancashire bilberry pie is made by adding a few mint leaves and soft brown sugar to the berries and using them to fill a double crust plate pie.

Bilberry jam

1·1 kg (2½ lb) bilberries
150 ml (¼ pint) water
45 ml (3 tbsp) lemon juice
1·4 kg (3 lb) sugar
a bottle of commercial pectin, eg. Certo*

Pick over the fruit, removing any leaves and stalks. Wash carefully, drain and put in a pan with the water and lemon juice. Simmer gently for about 10–15 minutes until the fruit is soft and just beginning to pulp. Add the sugar, stir until dissolved, then bring to the boil; boil for 3 minutes. Remove from heat, add the pectin and boil for a further minute. Allow to cool slightly before potting and covering in the usual way.
Yield: about 2·5 kg (5½ lb)

* Available from supermarkets

Bilberry jelly

1·4 kg (3 lb) bilberries
1·4 kg (3 lb) cooking apples
water to cover
90 ml (6 tbsp) lemon juice
sugar

Wash the fruit, remove the bilberry stalks and slice the apples without peeling or coring. Put all the fruit in a saucepan, barely cover with water, add the lemon juice and cook until tender. Crush the bilberries, if necessary, then strain the pulp through a jelly bag. Measure the extract, return to the pan with 450 g (1 lb) sugar to each 600 ml (1 pint) of extract. When the sugar has dissolved, boil rapidly until setting point is reached. Skim, pot and cover in the usual way.

Blackberry One of the 400 species of blackberry or bramble is to be found in most parts of Britain. The pale pinky white flowers are a common sight along the roadsides and hedges in spring and in summer the large clusters of glossy black berries are recognised by everybody. Eat the first berries – the pick of the crop – raw with sugar and fresh cream or ice cream. Take home plenty more to turn into the ever popular blackberry and apple pie or crumble; or try bramble jelly; blackberry and apple jam, jelly or chutney. You can even make a cordial or wine. While on holiday, try these simple but delicious recipes, using fruit picked straight from the bush.

♨ Blackberry fool

Stew the berries gently in a saucepan with enough water to cover the base of the pan, until just tender. Mash the fruit with a wooden spoon or sieve if you prefer. Stir the pulp into an equal quantity of cold custard or whipped cream. Sweeten to taste and cool before serving.

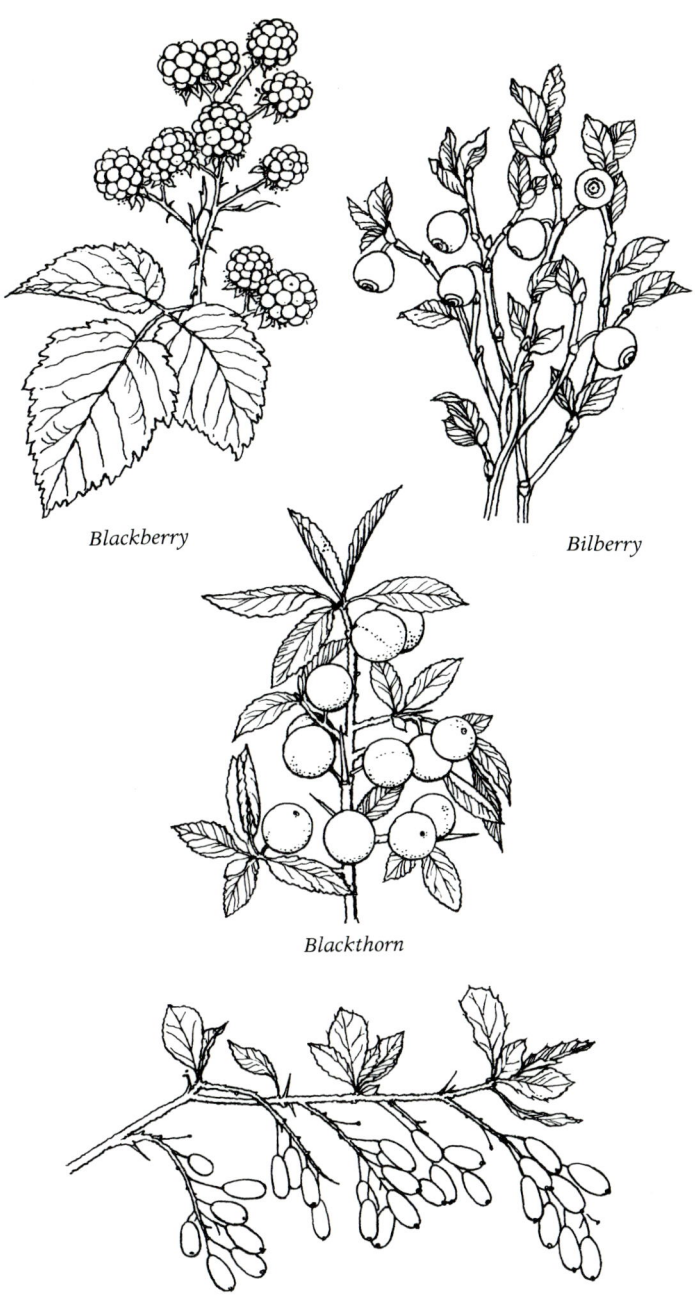

Blackberry

Bilberry

Blackthorn

Common barberry

Blackberry salad

This is a very old idea but certainly simple to make on a sunny day and delicious to eat. Pick only the very large berries, place them in a glass bowl in the heat of the sun and leave them to warm through. Lightly crush the fruit, add sugar to taste and a little red wine.

♨ Bramble syllabub

325 g (12 oz) blackberries
15 ml (1 level tbsp) sugar
2·5 ml ($\frac{1}{2}$ level tsp) ground mace (optional)
2 egg whites
100 g (4 oz) caster sugar
juice of $\frac{1}{2}$ lemon
150 ml ($\frac{1}{4}$ pint) dry white wine
284-ml (10-fl oz) carton of double cream, whipped

If you have picked plenty of blackberries and feel like indulging in a special pud – try this super Bramble syllabub.

Pick over and wash the blackberries, dry them well. Put in a pan with 15 ml (1 level tbsp) sugar and mace and cook gently, until the fruit is soft. Allow to cool and divide between four serving dishes. Stir the caster sugar, lemon juice, wine and whipped cream together. Whisk the egg whites stiffly and fold into the cream mixture. Spoon the mixture over the fruit. Chill, if possible, before serving.

Blackthorn This very prickly shrub which produces the sloe is often found in great thickets on open grasslands. You'll find the best crops of berries in southern coastal areas where late frosts don't destroy the snow-white blossoms. The blossom appears on leafless boughs in April and is succeeded in autumn by the blue black sloe berries which have a powdery bloom on their skins. The berries are rather like small plums. They have an astringent flavour and are probably best known as the distinctive flavour in sloe gin. You can also make them into wine, jams and jellies.

Sloe and apple jelly

1·8 kg (4 lb) cooking apples
900 g (2 lb) sloes
water to cover
sugar

Wash the fruit, removing the stalks, and chop the apples without peeling or coring. Put all the fruit in a saucepan and just cover with water. Simmer gently until the fruit is tender. Strain the fruit through a jelly bag overnight. Measure the juice, return to the pan with 450 g (1 lb) sugar to each 600 ml (1 pint) of juice. When the sugar has dissolved, boil rapidly until setting point is reached. Skim, pot and cover in the usual way.
Yield: about 2·7 kg (6 lb)

Sloe gin

450 g (1 lb) sloes
75–100 g (3–4 oz) granulated sugar
almond essence
900 ml (1½ pints) undiluted gin

Stalk and clean the sloes, prick all over with a darning needle and put into a screw-top jar. Add the sugar and a few drops of almond essence. Fill up the bottle with the gin, screw down tightly and leave in a dark place for 3 months, shaking occasionally. At the end of this time, open the jar and strain through muslin until clear. Re-bottle, cork and leave until required.

Common barberry You may find this deciduous shrub growing in hedges throughout Britain, though in recent years it has become rather scarce. In spring it has clusters of bright yellow flowers and in autumn clusters of tiny bright red berries. The sharp acid fruit may be used instead of redcurrants to make jam or jelly or instead of cranberries to make a sharp, fruit sauce to serve with meat.

Crab apple There are many species, ranging from trees with thorny branches yielding small, sour fruit to larger pleasant-tasting ones – the sour ones make the best jelly, the larger ones may be eaten raw. You can recognise the tree by its oval leaves, which look just like the cultivated variety. The apples grow in clusters and are ripe as soon as they start turning bright red. They make delicious jelly and jam.

Crab apple jelly

2·7 kg (6 lb) crab apples
2·3 litres (4 pints) water
cloves or bruised root ginger (optional)
sugar

Wash and quarter the crab apples, without peeling or coring. Put them into a saucepan and add the water. Bring to the boil and simmer for about $1\frac{1}{2}$ hours, or until the fruit is pulped, adding a little more water if necessary. A few cloves or bruised root ginger may be added, while the apples are cooking, to give extra flavour. Strain through a jelly bag. Measure the extract, return it to the pan with 450 g (1 lb) sugar to each 600 ml (1 pint) of extract. Bring to the boil, stirring until the sugar has dissolved, then boil rapidly until setting point is reached. Skim, pot and cover in the usual way.

Crab apple butter

1·4 kg (3 lb) crab apples
water or water and cider to cover
2·5 ml ($\frac{1}{2}$ level tsp) ground cinnamon
2·5 ml ($\frac{1}{2}$ level tsp) ground cloves
sugar

Wash and chop the apples without peeling or coring. Place in a pan, just cover with the liquid and simmer gently until really soft and pulpy. Sieve and weigh the pulp, return it to the pan with the spices and 325 g (12 oz) sugar to each 450 g (1 lb) of pulp. Stir until the sugar dissolves, then boil gently, stirring

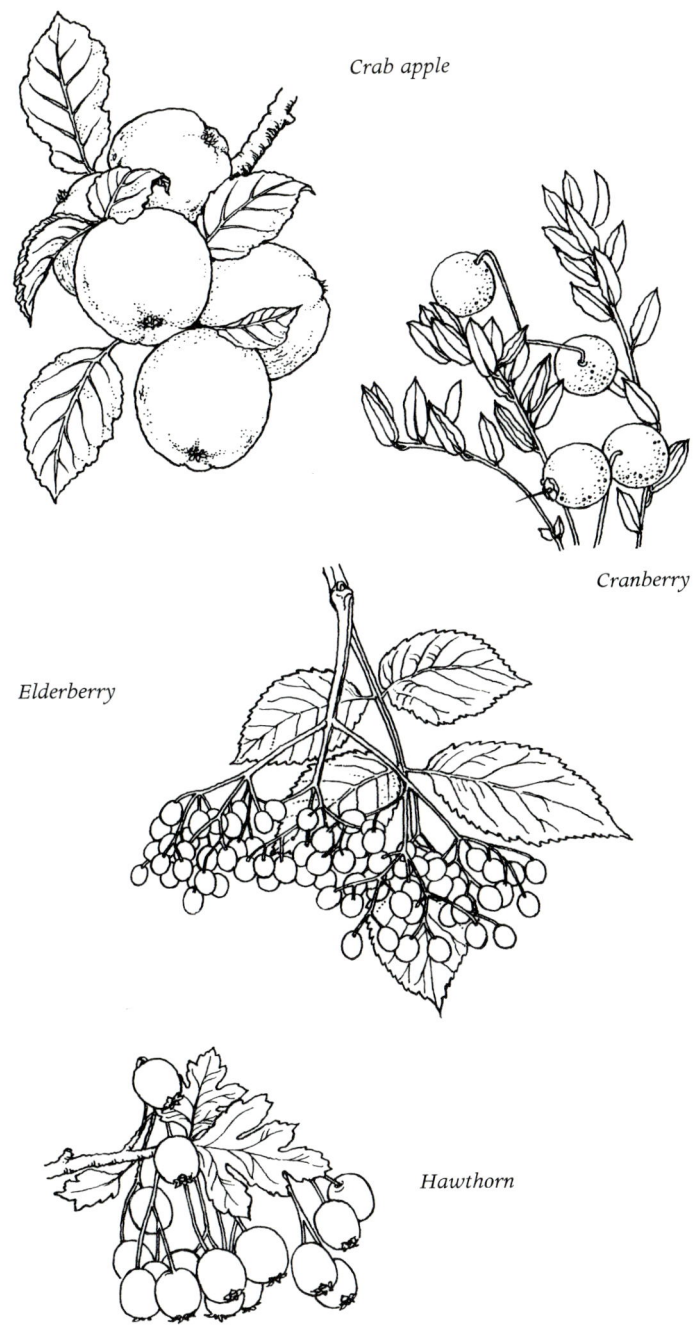

Crab apple

Cranberry

Elderberry

Hawthorn

regularly, until creamy in consistency. Pour into small jars and cover as for jam. Serve as a spread.

Cranberry The cranberry comes from a low growing plant that grows best in a wet, open environment. At one time it grew all over Britain but reclamation of land and improved soil drainage has now made it less common in the south. The plant has small dark shiny leaves and the fruit ripens between July and August. Wild cranberries are yellow with red speckles – the red is brighter in colour than the berries we are used to seeing in the shops at Christmas time. The berries are too acid and sharp to eat raw but can be made into the traditional cranberry sauce or cheese, jams and jellies.

Cranberry cheese

700 g (1½ lb) cranberries
900 ml (1½ pints) water
700 g (1½ lb) sugar

Wash and pick over the cranberries, put into a saucepan with the water and simmer until tender, adding a little more water, if necessary. When cooked rub through a sieve with a wooden spoon. Wash out the pan, return the purée with the sugar and bring to the boil, stirring continuously. Boil until a semi-solid consistency is reached. Pot and cover in the usual way. Serve with roast turkey or cold meats.

Cranberry and apple jam

700 g (1½ lb) cranberries
700 g (1½ lb) cooking apples
300 ml (½ pint) water
1·4 kg (3 lb) sugar

Wash the cranberries and peel, core and slice the apples. Place the fruit in a saucepan with the water. Simmer gently for 15 minutes or until the fruit is tender. Add the sugar, stirring until dissolved and the mixture comes to the boil. Boil rapidly for about 10 minutes or until the setting point is reached. Pot and cover in the usual way.

Yield: about 2·3 kg (5 lb)

Elderberry The fruits and flowers of the elder tree have been used by country people all over Britain for many years for winemaking. The heavily scented, cream coloured flower clusters that appear in summer can be used to flavour wine, to make into an astringent water ice, or, in small quantities, to flavour jam or jelly. Make a muscat-flavoured gooseberry jam by adding 3–4 elderflower heads, tied in a muslin bag, to each 450 g (1 lb) of berries. Add to the pan with the sugar but remove the heads before potting. If you are feeling adventurous, try green elderberry stalks, skinned then cooked in the same way as asparagus by standing upright in boiling, salted water and simmering gently until tender. The berries are blue black in colour, and grow in largish clusters. They are ripe when the heads turn down, and very popular with blackbirds and starlings – so you will have to be quick to get there first!

Use really ripe berries to fill a single crust pie. Sweeten the berries with brown sugar or golden syrup, add 2–3 cloves and a little water, cover with a pastry crust and bake in the normal way. Once you've tried it you may well prefer elderberry pie to a blackcurrant pie. Use the same mixture to fill a suet pudding or top it with a sponge mixture to steam or bake. While on holiday stew really ripe elderberries with a little water and sugar to taste and serve hot with custard or cold with cream. Pick plenty more to take home and make into Elderberry jelly.

Elderberry jelly

900 g (2 lb) elderberries
900 g (2 lb) cooking apples
water to cover
sugar

Wash and pick over the elderberries. Wash the apples and

chop roughly without peeling or coring. Cook the two fruits separately, with just enough water to cover, until both are really soft and pulped. Combine the fruit and strain it through a jelly bag. Measure the extract and return it to the pan with 450 g (1 lb) sugar to each 600 ml (1 pint) of extract. Bring to the boil, stirring until the sugar has dissolved, then boil rapidly until setting point is reached. Skim, pot and cover in the usual way.

Hawthorn One of Britain's commonest wild hedge shrubs found particularly on commonland. In spring it bears the familiar May blossom and in autumn clusters of small crimson haws. The blossom can be turned into a potent liqueur by adding a handful of clean petals to brandy and leaving to mature for 3 months. In summer, pick the small, tight green buds before they begin to open and add them to potato or beetroot salad. Gather the ripe, red haws in autumn to make into jelly or jam, adding cooking apples or crab apples for extra pectin.

Hawthorn potato salad

225 g (8 oz) cooked potatoes
50 g (2 oz) fresh hawthorn buds (see above)
1 small onion, skinned and finely chopped
salad cream or mayonnaise
salt and freshly ground pepper

Cut the potatoes into 1-cm ($\frac{1}{2}$-in) cubes. Wash and chop the hawthorn buds. Combine all the ingredients together, adding enough salad cream or mayonnaise to coat the potatoes. Cover and leave in a cool place for 30 minutes or so for the flavours to blend together.

Juniper You will find this tall wild evergreen shrub in clumps on the chalk downs of southern England, in the Lake

District and parts of the Scottish Highlands. Small berries appear on the bush remain green for about two years before ripening and turning blue black. Ripe berries have a strong pine-like aroma. Crush them to release the flavour and use them fresh or dried in stuffings for game, pork or mutton or in casseroles of game, pork, mutton or lamb.

Rose hip Wild roses grow in hedges all over Britain; their colour varies from white to deep pink. The fruit or 'hip' that develops once the flower has died is amber red in colour, with hairy seeds inside which makes it unpleasant to eat raw. Rose hips are famous for their high vitamin C content – hence the commercially made syrup. You can make your own syrup or jam when you get home if you gather the hips when they are deep red and fully ripe but not soft. Split them, remove the seeds or pips and cook them according to the recipe. While on holiday make the hips into a tasty sauce to serve with ice cream, fruit or jelly.

Rose hip sauce

450 g (1 lb) rose hips
water
30 ml (2 level tbsp) sugar
a little wine or cider (optional)
cornflour to thicken

Wash the hips and remove the stalks, top and seeds. Put in a saucepan with a little water and cook gently until tender and pulpy. Sieve the hips and return to the pan with the sugar (adding more sugar if required) and wine or cider. Heat gently until the sugar dissolves, stirring occasionally. Blend the cornflour with a little cold water to a smooth paste, add to the sauce, bring to the boil and continue cooking, stirring continuously, until the sauce thickens.

Rose hip syrup

900 g (2 lb) rose hips
1·7 litres (3 pints) boiling water
450 g (1 lb) sugar

Mince or finely chop the hips and put them at once into the
boiling water. Bring back to boiling point, remove the
saucepan from the heat and leave it to stand for 10–15 minutes.
Strain through a clean cloth or jelly bag. When it stops
dripping, return the pulp in the bag to the pan with another
900 ml (1½ pints) boiling water and reserve the extracted juice.
Reboil the pulp and water, allow to stand as before and strain.
Mix the two extracts together, pour into a clean pan and reduce
by boiling, until the juice measures 900 ml (1½ pints). Add the
sugar, stirring until dissolved, and boil for 5 minutes. Pour the
syrup into hot clean bottles and seal at once.

Sterilise the bottles by placing in a deep pan padded with
thick cloth or newspaper. Fill the pan up to the bottle necks with
warm water. Heat the water to simmering point and maintain
this temperature for 20 minutes. Remove the bottles and cool.
Store in a cool, dry place.

Rowan or mountain ash This tree is common in the Scottish
Highlands but you may also find it in sandy areas of England.
The creamy flowers appear in May and clusters of berries ripen
from early August onwards. The berries should be really ripe
and bright red before being picked but don't leave them until
the skins shrivel. They are too astringent to eat raw but you can
make a wine or jelly that is delicious eaten with game, venison
or fatty meats, such as pork.

Rowan jelly

1·8 kg (4 lb) ripe rowan berries
900 ml (1½ pints) water
60 ml (4 tbsp) lemon juice
sugar

Remove the stems from the berries and wash them. Put into a

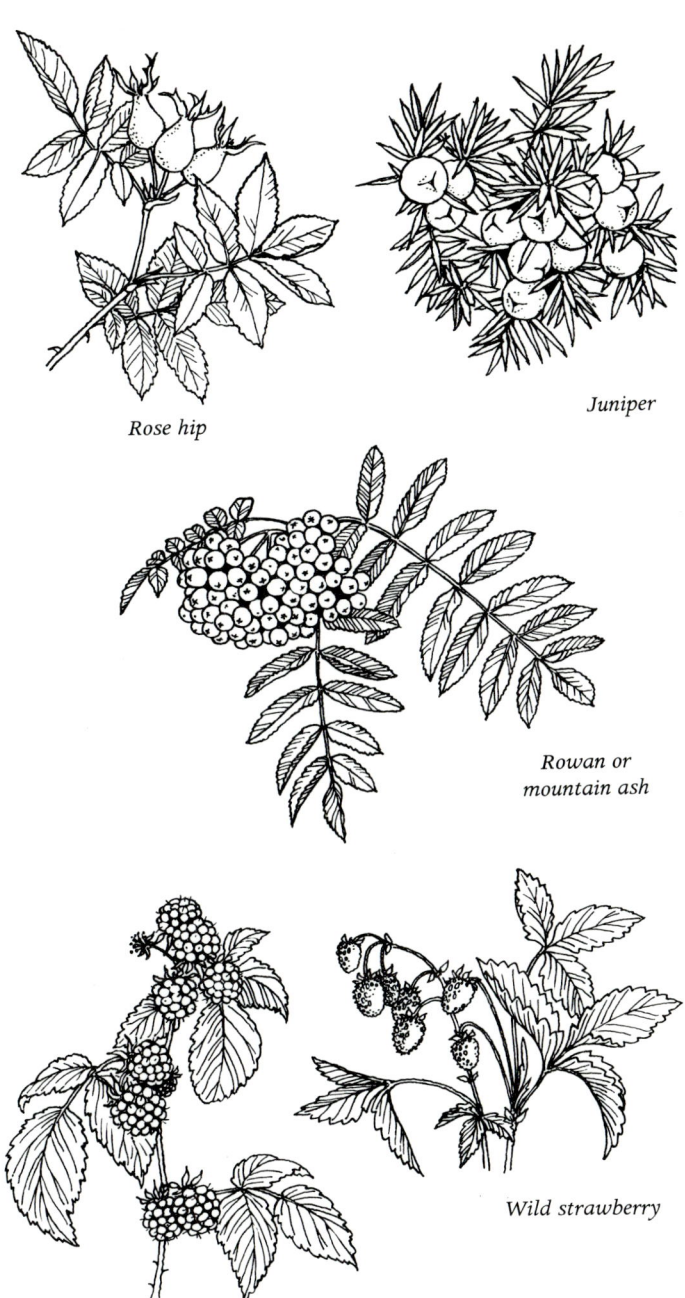

Rose hip

Juniper

*Rowan or
mountain ash*

Wild raspberry

Wild strawberry

saucepan with water and lemon juice. Bring to the boil and simmer gently for $\frac{3}{4}$–1 hour to extract the juice, then strain through a jelly bag. Measure the extract, return to the pan and bring to the boil. Remove the pan from the heat, add 450 g (1 lb) sugar to each 600 ml (1 pint) of juice and stir until dissolved. Bring to the boil and boil rapidly until the setting point is reached. Skim and pot in the usual way.

Wild raspberry You'll find this on heaths and open woodlands, particularly in Scotland. Wild plants have shorter canes than the cultivated variety. Flowers appear from June to August, followed by red or yellow fruit, usually smaller than cultivated raspberries but with a very rich flavour. If you can manage to pick enough fruit without succumbing to the temptation of eating it as you go, wild raspberries make a delicious dessert eaten raw, sprinkled with a little caster sugar, and plenty of fresh cream. If the fruit is very tiny, crush the berries and mix them with an equal quantity of whipped cream or custard and sweeten to taste for a quick raspberry fool – or try the recipe below. Wild raspberries also make very good jam.

☖ Raspberry honey sundae

Layer wild raspberries, ice cream or whipped cream with chopped nuts in glass dishes. Pour cooled honey sauce (see below) over the top, decorate with more whipped cream and serve with shortbread biscuits. To make honey sauce: melt 50 g (2 oz) butter in a small pan. Stir in 7·5 ml (1½ level tsp) cornflour and 60 ml (4 tbsp) thin honey. Bring to the boil, stirring and cook for a minute or two.

Wild strawberry All the cultivated strawberries grown today originated from the wild or wood strawberry. In developing the larger sized fruit some of the flavour has been lost – once you have sampled wild strawberries you will appreciate the difference. Look for wild strawberries in woods and thickets, sometimes on banks near ditches, between June and September. Pick only the ripened fruits, wash carefully and serve sprinkled with caster sugar and fresh cream. If you are lucky enough to find plenty of plants and tire of eating them simply (an unlikely event!), try serving them with cheesecake, or stirred into yoghurt, or crushed and made into milk shake or the fruit cup below.

Wild strawberry cup

100 g (4 oz) wild strawberries
50 g (2 oz) caster sugar
1 bottle dry white wine or cider

This makes a lovely refreshing drink for a hot summer evening.

   Sprinkle the strawberries with sugar, pour half the wine over them, cover and leave in a cool place for 30 minutes. Add the remaining wine and serve in tall glasses with ice if possible. A splash of soda will add bubbles if you are using dry wine.

Strawberry froth

225 g (8 oz) ripe strawberries, hulled
1 egg white
75 g (3 oz) icing or caster sugar

Do not wash the strawberries – wipe them if necessary. Put the berries into a bowl and squash them. Add the egg white and sugar and whisk for about 10 minutes, until thick and frothy. Turn into glass dishes and serve with single cream.

FISH

Although the idea of fishing for the family's supper is quite romantic, it is not as easy as all that these days, because all stretches of inland water are controlled by the water board or privately owned and can only be fished with a licence – if at all. Even if you possess a licence the number of fish you can take home with you is usually limited and the fish must be above a certain weight – if you're lucky enough to catch anything at all! However, if you are holidaying near the coast, there are no restrictions to the amount of fish you can take from the sea or buy from the local fishermen. The fish you are most likely to catch, off the pier or near the beaches if you hire a small boat are: mackerel, herring, pilchards, dabs and sprats.

Mackerel A beautiful long, slender fish with a blue and green striped back, silvery underside and firm flesh. It deteriorates quickly and should be eaten as fresh as possible, preferably on the day of catching. Treat the small fish like trout and grill or fry in butter. If you catch a larger one, split, stuff and bake it, mixing the soft roe with the stuffing and baking the hard roe underneath the fish. Mackerel should not be boiled or stewed as this loses flavour. The season lasts from October to July, but the fish is at its best in April, May and June.

Grilled or fried mackerel

Cut off the heads and fins, clean the fish but leave whole. Wash and wipe them. Make 2–3 diagonal cuts in the flesh on both sides of the fish and sprinkle with salt and pepper. Brush with oil or melted butter and cook under a hot grill or in a frying pan for 10–15 minutes each side, turning once. Serve with mustard or with horseradish sauce.

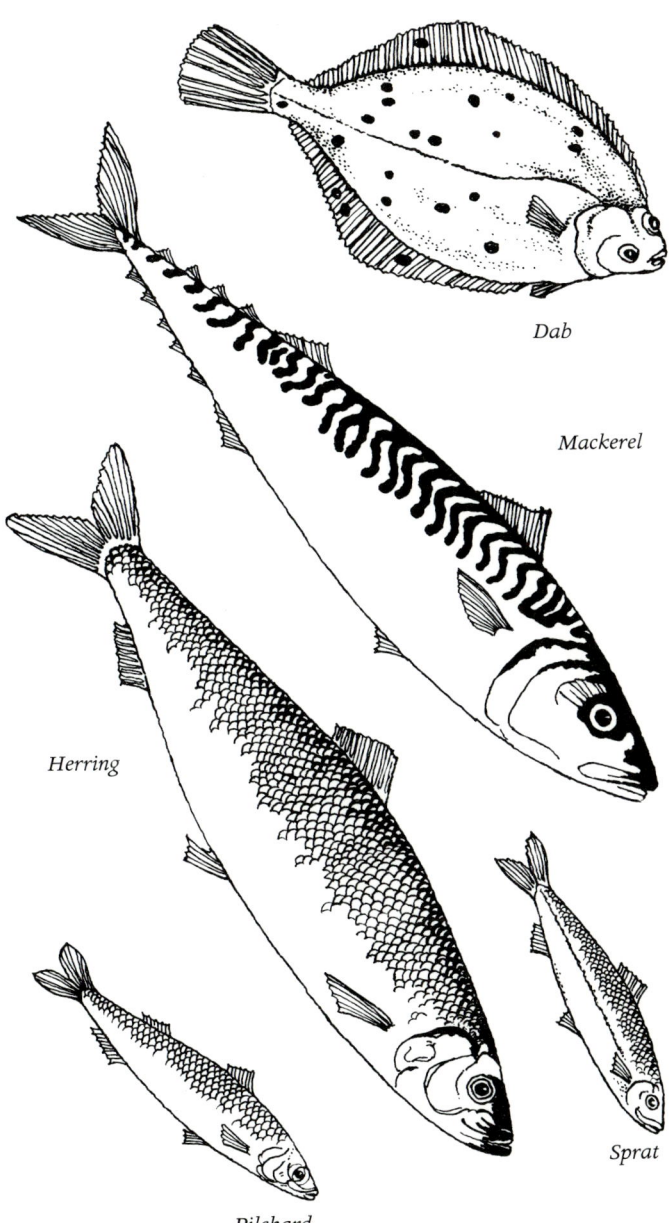

Dab

Mackerel

Herring

Sprat

Pilchard

Orange stuffed mackerel

4 mackerel, cleaned

For the stuffing
1 large orange, peeled
$\frac{1}{4}$ onion, skinned and finely chopped
50 g (2 oz) fresh white breadcrumbs
dried parsley (optional)
juice of 1 lemon
salt and pepper

Trim off the heads and tails, wash and wipe the fish and remove the backbones (see below). Chop the flesh of the orange and mix with the onion, crumbs, parsley, if used, lemon juice and seasoning. Fill the fish with the stuffing and place them in a frying pan. Add 150 ml ($\frac{1}{4}$ pint) water, cover and simmer gently for 20–30 minutes, until the fish are tender. Drain and serve with salad.

To remove the backbone from mackerel or herring:
Place the split fish, skin side up, on a board and lightly press down the middle of the back to loosen the bone. Turn the fish over and ease the backbone up.

Herring A small, delicately flavoured fish, usually weighing about 175 g (6 oz). It has silvery blue scales on the back and a silvery belly. The flesh is firm and creamy brown in colour and the fish is best fried or grilled, although it is quite often preserved commercially by smoking or pickling. The herring is at its best from June to March, although it is in season all year round.

If you are lucky enough to sample local pickled or smoked herrings, you will need to know what is what:

Bismark herring herring fillet, marinaded in spiced vinegar with onion rings.

Bloater lightly smoked and salted. It must be grilled or fried on the day of purchase as it does not keep well.

Buckling whole smoked herring that requires no cooking.

Kipper split herring soaked in brine before smoking. Usually sold in pairs. Grill or poach.

Rollmop herring fillet marinaded in spiced vinegar, rolled around chopped onion, gherkins and peppercorns.

Salt herring whole or gutted, preserved in heavy salt brine. Soak for 24 hours before eating.

An English recipe of 1840

'Take fresh Yarmouth bloaters, cut off the heads and tails and open the herring down the back; grill over a red fire on a grid iron. Rub over with a lump of cold butter, sprinkle with black pepper and serve plain, smoking hot, with thick bread.'

Grilled or fried herrings

Follow the recipe for Grilled or fried mackerel (see page 144).

Fried herrings in oatmeal

Remove the heads, tails and fins and bone the herrings (see page 146). Clean the flesh by rubbing with a little salt, then rinse and dry well. Sprinkle with salt and pepper and coat with fine oatmeal, pressing it well into the fish on both sides. Fry in a small amount of oil or butter in a frying pan, turning the fish once, until brown, 10–15 minutes on each side. Drain well on kitchen paper and serve with lemon wedges.

Pilchard A very small fish, with a delicate flavour, similar to the herring. It has a blue black back and a silvery belly. Pilchards are most commonly caught off the coast of Devon and Cornwall and, as they deteriorate quickly, should be eaten the day they are caught. To cook, grill or fry pilchards whole.

If you are holidaying in Cornwall, sample its famous Stargazey pie. This recipe was developed many years ago because cooks considered it a waste of pastry to cover the inedible heads and tail, although the head couldn't be removed as the rich fish oils would be lost. The fish are arranged in the pie so the oil runs back into the flesh and keeps the fish moist while cooking.

Dab A flat fish related to the plaice but smaller, with rough, scaly skin and white flesh. It is excellent either fried or baked, whole or cut into fillets.

Sprat Small, silvery skinned fish of the herring family, smaller than the sardine. As it is difficult to skin and bone it is usually grilled or fried whole.

☖ Fried sprats

To prepare sprats for cooking, make a small cut with scissors just below the gills and gently press out the entrails, leaving the heads on. Wash the fish thoroughly and dry well. Toss the whole fish in seasoned flour and fry in hot oil or butter for 4–5 minutes, until golden brown.

FUNGI

Field mushrooms freshly picked and still moist from the early morning dew are a delight that can rarely be enjoyed, unless you are on holiday or live near a field where mushrooms grow. Only pick fungi if you know which is which or have an illustrated guide with you, for confident identification. Don't take chances and, if you are unsure, leave them alone. Beware particularly of the dangerous Death cap fungus which you will recognise because it is pure white all over – even the gills – and tends to grow singly. Eat gathered mushrooms or fungi as fresh as possible. Use either common field mushrooms, horse mushrooms or puff balls for the recipes below.

Common field mushroom Can be eaten at two stages in its growth – either as a 'button' mushroom, when it has just risen from the spawn and is still quite white, or when it begins to grow and the stalk lengthens, the top flattens, exposing rosy-pink gills underneath. As these gills turn brown and even

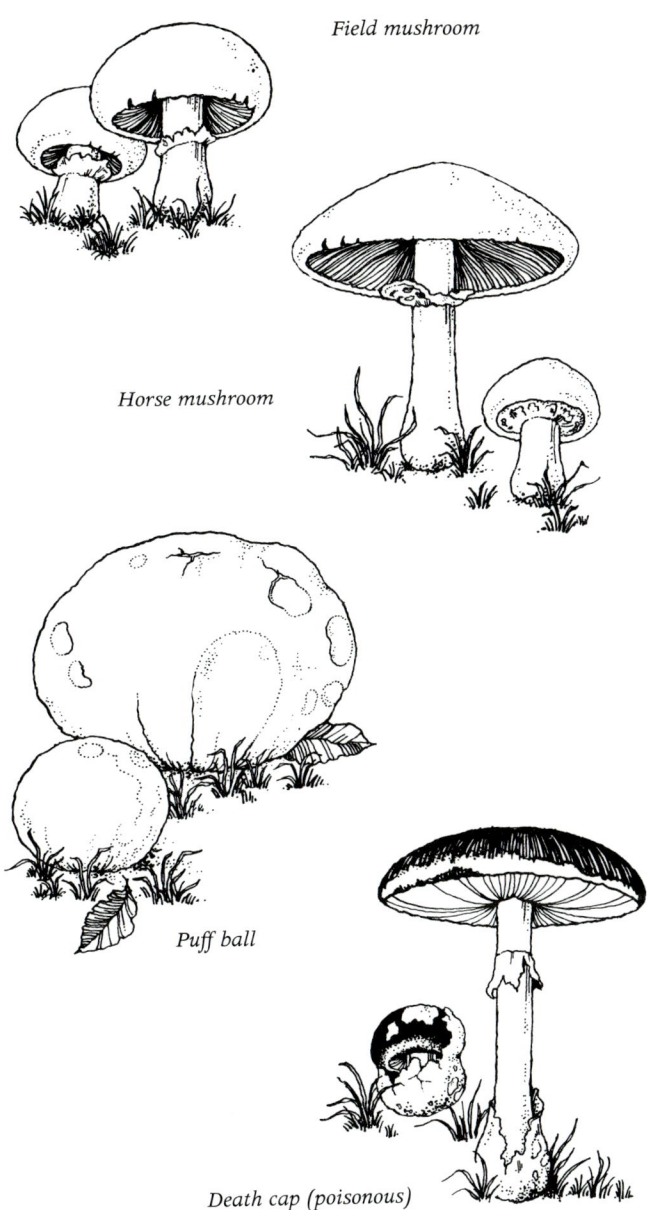

Field mushroom

Horse mushroom

Puff ball

Death cap (poisonous)

black, it means the mushroom is getting over-ripe and should be left alone. Also avoid maggoty, sloppy mushrooms or ones which have become water-logged with rain. Field mushrooms grow in open fields, quite often where cattle or horses graze. They can grow up to 60 cm (24 in) across. The average size is 10–15 cm (4–6 in) across, but the smaller mushrooms have a more delicate flavour.

Horse mushroom This is a larger, clumsier version of the field mushroom and can be recognised by its thicker cap and lumpy stem. To test that your find is a horse mushroom and not another unpleasant-tasting (though not poisonous) relation, cut or bruise the cap. If it is a definite yellow mustard-colour inside, discard it. The horse mushroom is a very firm fungus, ideal to stuff, grill with bacon, bake or serve filled with scrambled egg or tomatoes.

Puff ball A descriptive name for a fungus which usually grows near common field or horse mushrooms: it looks like a ball of smooth white cream cheese and when you touch it the outer skin is as fine as kid leather. Only eat young puff balls, as the inside turns a yellowy, green brown colour as it grows older. The delicate flavour is beautifully enhanced if puff balls are gently poached in milk. They can be fried in butter and the larger puff balls can be sliced, coated in beaten egg and crumbs, fried in butter and served with a slice of lemon.

Creamed mushrooms

225 g (8 oz) mushrooms
300 ml (½ pint) milk
25 ml (1½ level tbsp) cornflour
knob of butter
15–30 ml (1–2 tbsp) cream
salt and pepper
lemon juice
4 slices of buttered toast

Simmer the mushrooms in a saucepan in most of the milk until just soft, about 10 minutes. Blend the cornflour to a smooth paste with the remaining milk. Add to the pan and bring to the boil, stirring, until the sauce thickens. Cook for 2–3 minutes, then stir in the butter, cream, seasoning and lemon juice. Serve on buttered toast.

Stuffed mushrooms

8 medium sized mushrooms
1 small onion, skinned and finely chopped
50 g (2 oz) butter
45 ml (3 level tbsp) finely chopped ham or cooked bacon
75 ml (5 level tbsp) fresh breadcrumbs
25 g (1 oz) cheese, grated or cut into small cubes
beaten egg to bind
salt and pepper
4 slices of buttered toast

Remove and chop the mushroom stalks. Lightly fry the stalks and onion in 25 g (1 oz) butter until soft, about 5 minutes. Add the ham, breadcrumbs, cheese and enough beaten egg to bind. Stir until well mixed and season to taste. Pile the mixture into the mushroom caps, dot with the remaining butter and cook under a hot grill for 15–20 minutes. Serve on toast.

Marinated mushrooms

450–700 g (1–1½ lb) button mushrooms
juice of 1 large lemon
300 ml (½ pint) wine vinegar
2 medium onions, skinned and chopped
1 bouquet garni (optional)
5 ml (1 level tsp) salt
freshly ground black pepper
300 ml (½ pint) vegetable oil
15 ml (1 level tbsp) tomato ketchup

Wipe the mushrooms, put them in a saucepan with the lemon juice and enough water to cover. Bring to the boil, boil for 5 minutes, remove from the heat then leave until cold. Put the vinegar in another saucepan, add the onion, bouquet garni, if used, and seasoning. Bring to the boil and boil uncovered for 5 minutes. Cool. Add the oil and ketchup. Drain the mushrooms well and put in a deep bowl, pour the dressing over them, cover and leave to marinade for several hours or overnight. Serve with the marinade and crusty French bread.

♨ Cream of mushroom soup

225 g (8 oz) mushrooms, sliced
1 small onion, skinned and sliced
300 ml ($\frac{1}{2}$ pint) chicken stock
25 g (1 oz) butter or margarine
45 ml (3 level tbsp) flour
400 ml ($\frac{3}{4}$ pint) milk
salt and pepper
45 ml (3 tbsp) cream or top of the milk (optional)

Cook the mushrooms and onion in the stock in a covered pan for about 30 minutes. Sieve if you wish. Melt the fat in a saucepan, stir in the flour and cook for 2 minutes. Remove the pan from the heat and gradually stir in the milk, bring to the boil, stirring, and cook until the sauce thickens. Add the mushrooms, onions and seasoning and simmer for 10–15 minutes. Stir in the cream and serve.

NUTS

If you are taking a late autumn holiday, you will have a super selection of wild nuts to choose from. Scan the hedgerows and trees for hazelnuts, cobs, filberts, chestnuts, and perhaps even walnuts. If you have gathered a hoard of nuts you can always take them home. They will store for several months and have all sorts of uses – try them in fruit salads, cakes, puddings and savouries. To gather nuts for storage, make sure they are quite dry and in good condition.

To store hazelnuts, cobnuts and filberts: tightly pack them

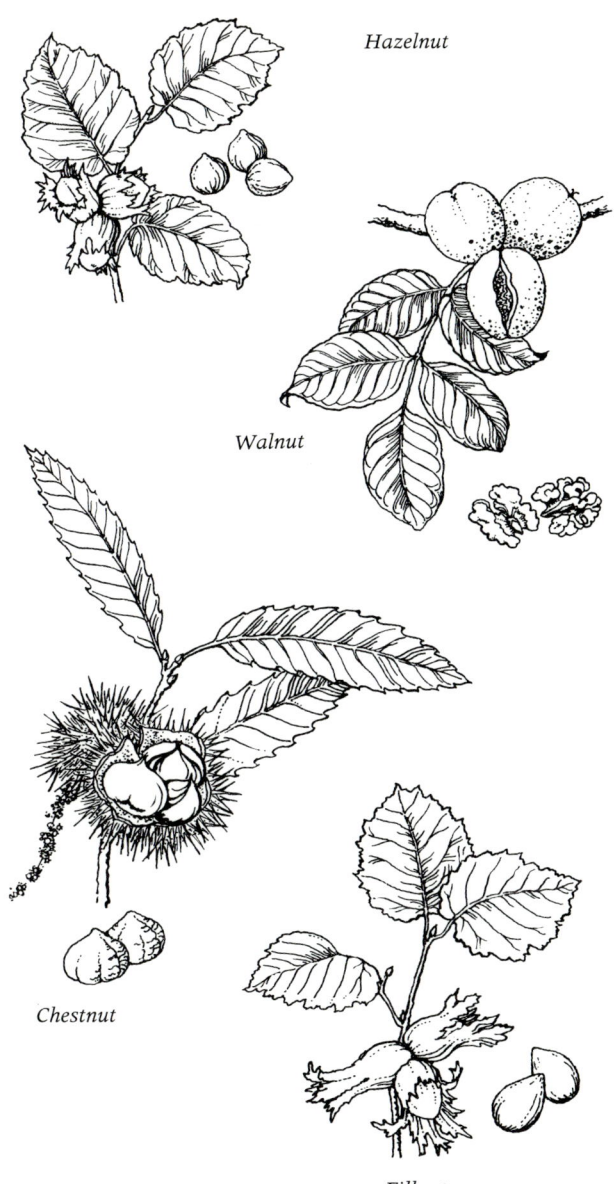

Hazelnut

Walnut

Chestnut

Filbert

into a jar to within 1·25-cm ($\frac{1}{2}$-in) of the top and cover with salt. Store in a cool, dry place.

To store walnuts and chestnuts: pack them into a box or crock with alternate layers of perfectly dry sand. Store in a cool, dry place. These are the most common varieties:

Hazelnut It is the most common nut in the British Isles and, although smaller than cultivated varieties, is sweeter if picked when fully grown but still green. Hazelnuts are not always easy to find as they are well hidden by leaves and of course, the best nuts are always just out of reach. Always go prepared with a walking stick or a long forked stick to pull down the higher branches. The nuts have a delicious milky taste when eaten raw or you can take them back to the caravan and sauté them, shelled and skinned, in butter. Sprinkle with salt or sugar and eat while still hot.

Kentish cob Similar to the hazelnut but much larger and round with a woody shell and short husks.

Filbert This is a variety of hazelnut, but the nut is longer, instead of nearly round. Unlike the hazelnut the filbert is completely covered by the husks.

Sweet chestnut You can distinguish it from the horse chestnut because the shell is less prickly and the nut flatter and less shiny. Sweet chestnuts can be eaten raw but as they are slightly bitter in taste they are perhaps better roasted, stewed or boiled, and, if you like, puréed.

Walnut If you are lucky enough to find a walnut tree, look out for the nuts in brown shells with a faint sheen. Avoid any that rattle, as the nut inside will be dry and shrivelled. Green or unripe walnuts may be eaten fresh but are usually pickled.

♨ Hazelnut and cheese fruit salad

200 g (7 oz) cream cheese
15 ml (1 level tbsp) raisins
30 ml (2 tbsp) chopped hazelnuts
4 large peach halves, fresh or canned
1 lettuce, washed

Beat the cheese until smooth. Put the raisins into boiling water for 1–2 minutes to soften them. Drain, cool and mix with half the nuts and the cheese. Arrange the peach halves on a bed of lettuce, hollow side up, fill each with a spoonful of the cheese and raisin mixture and sprinkle with the remaining nuts.

Raisin and nut salad

2 sharp eating apples
100 g (4 oz) raisins, chopped
50 g (2 oz) walnuts or hazelnuts
salad dressing
1 bunch of watercress, washed and trimmed

Wipe the apples but do not peel; grate or chop them into a bowl. Add the raisins and nuts and coat with salad dressing. Arrange the watercress on a serving plate and top with the apple and nut mixture.

LOCALLY GROWN FOOD

While touring round the country keep an eye out for food that has been grown locally and can be purchased straight from the farmer, orchard, local market or roadside stall. It'll not only be cheaper – but fresher too. During the height of summer when so many fruits and vegetables are being harvested some farmers allow you to come and 'pick your own' for a very reasonable price – this applies particularly to strawberries and the other soft fruits – raspberries, blackcurrants and red-currants. Alternatively, if you're looking for an energetic open air holiday with a bonus thrown in, look out for places advertising 'fruit-picking holidays'. The grower usually offers a free caravan park and 'pocket money' in return for a fixed number of hours picking per day – quite often just the morning. If, at the end of the week or fortnight of picking apples, pears or whatever, you are still keen to buy in bulk, the farmer will usually offer fruit at discount or competitive prices.

Make a point of visiting local markets – not only are they great hunting grounds for good buys but you will also get to meet the local people. The friendly atmosphere at a country market is enchanting and most entertaining, particularly if the local cattle, sheep or pig auctions are held on the same day. At the market you will often find first class fruit and vegetables grown locally and brought to the stalls early that morning, in the peak of condition. Also look out for home produced honey, eggs, plants and flowers. And if there's a Women's Institute stall you may be lucky enough to find delicious home made preserves and home baked cakes, biscuits and pies. If you can afford it, take the opportunity to buy in bulk fruit and vegetables that store well so you can reap the benefit the rest of the year:

Potatoes can be stored in hessian sacks or large perforated paper or plastic bags.

Onions should be stored so air can circulate around them – either in slatted trays or open weave sacks or, if the tops have not been cut, why not make your own onion strings.

Carrots should be layered in boxes of damp sand and kept in a cool, dry, frost-proof place.

Apples and pears should be wrapped individually in newspaper and arranged in slatted trays or boxes so the fruit does not touch. Check them regularly and remove any decaying fruit.

If you are holidaying on the coast seek out the local fish stalls where you can buy freshly caught fish, especially herring, mackerel, dabs and shellfish, at very reasonable prices. Quite often small fishing vessels will sell their catch straight from the boats so always investigate harbours towards the end of the afternoon or early in the morning – local folk always know when the boats are expected! Obviously, fish bought straight from the boat couldn't be fresher but if you are buying from a fish stall always check that the fish *are* really fresh – they should have firm even-textured flesh, clear, full, shiny eyes, bright red gills and a clean smell.

Index